Too Much *and*
Never Enough

Too Much *and* Never Enough

HOW MY FAMILY
CREATED THE WORLD'S
MOST DANGEROUS MAN

Mary L. Trump

**SIMON &
SCHUSTER**

London · New York · Sydney · Toronto · New Delhi

First published in the United States by Simon & Schuster Inc., 2020
First published in Great Britain by Simon & Schuster UK Ltd, 2020

5 7 9 10 8 6 4

Simon & Schuster UK Ltd
1st Floor
222 Gray's Inn Road
London WC1X 8HB

www.simonandschuster.co.uk
www.simonandschuster.com.au
www.simonandschuster.co.in

Simon & Schuster Australia, Sydney
Simon & Schuster India, New Delhi

The author and publishers have made all reasonable efforts to contact
copyright-holders for permission, and apologise for any omissions or errors
in the form of credits given. Corrections may be made to future printings.

A CIP catalogue record for this book
is available from the British Library

ISBN: 978-1-4711-9014-8

Interior design by Paul Dippolito
Printed and bound in Australia by Griffin Press, part of Ovato

MIX
Paper from
responsible sources
FSC
www.fsc.org   FSC® C009448

For my daughter, Avary,
and
my dad

If the soul is left in darkness, sins will be committed. The guilty one is not he who commits the sin, but the one who causes the darkness.

—Victor Hugo, *Les Misérables*

Contents

Author's Note

Much of this book comes from my own memory. For events during which I was not present, I relied on conversations and interviews, many of which are recorded, with members of my family, family friends, neighbors, and associates. I've reconstructed some dialogue according to what I personally remember and what others have told me. Where dialogue appears, my intention was to re-create the essence of conversations rather than provide verbatim quotes. I have also relied on legal documents, bank statements, tax returns, private journals, family documents, correspondence, emails, texts, photographs, and other records.

For general background, I relied on the *New York Times*, in particular the investigative article by David Barstow, Susanne Craig, and Russ Buettner that was published on October 2, 2018; the *Washington Post*; *Vanity Fair*; *Politico*; the TWA Museum website; and Norman Vincent Peale's *The Power of Positive Thinking*. For background on Steeplechase Park, I thank the Coney Island History Project website, *Brooklyn Paper*, and a May 14, 2018, article on 6sqft.com by Dana Schulz. For his insights into "the episodic man," thank you to Dan P. McAdams. For family history and information regarding Trump family businesses and alleged crimes, I am grateful for the reporting of the late Wayne Barrett, David Corn, Michael D'Antonio, David Cay Johnston, Tim O'Brien, Charles P. Pierce, and Adam Serwer. Thanks also to Gwenda Blair, and Michael Kranish and Marc Fisher—but my dad was forty-two, not forty-three, when he died.

Prologue

I'd always liked my name. As a kid at sailing camp in the 1970s, everybody called me Trump. It was a source of pride, not because the name was associated with power and real estate (back then my family was unknown outside of Brooklyn and Queens) but because something about the sound of it suited me, a tough six-year-old, afraid of nothing. In the 1980s, when I was in college and my uncle Donald had started branding all of his buildings in Manhattan, my feelings about my name became more complicated.

Thirty years later, on April 4, 2017, I was in the quiet car of an Amtrak train headed to Washington, DC, for a family dinner at the White House. Ten days earlier I had received an email inviting me to a birthday celebration for my aunts Maryanne, turning eighty, and Elizabeth, turning seventy-five. Their younger brother Donald had occupied the Oval Office since January.

After I emerged into Union Station, with its vaulted ceilings and black-and-white marble floors, I passed a vendor who had set up an easel with buttons for sale: my name in a red circle with a red slash through it, "DEPORT TRUMP," "DUMP TRUMP," and "TRUMP IS A WITCH." I put on my sunglasses and picked up my pace.

I took a cab to the Trump International Hotel, which was comping my family for one night. After checking in, I walked through the atrium and looked up at the glass ceiling and the blue sky beyond. The three-tiered crystal chandeliers that hung from the central beam of interconnected girders arching overhead cast a soft light. On one side,

armchairs, settees, and couches—royal blue, robin's-egg blue, ivory—
were arranged in small groups; on the other, tables and chairs circled
a large bar where I was later scheduled to meet my brother. I had expected the hotel to be vulgar and gilded. It wasn't.

My room was also tasteful. But my name was plastered everywhere,
on everything: TRUMP shampoo, TRUMP conditioner, TRUMP
slippers, TRUMP shower cap, TRUMP shoe polish, TRUMP sewing
kit, and TRUMP bathrobe. I opened the refrigerator, grabbed a split of
TRUMP white wine, and poured it down my Trump throat so it could
course through my Trump bloodstream and hit the pleasure center of
my Trump brain.

An hour later I met my brother, Frederick Crist Trump, III, whom
I've called Fritz since we were kids, and his wife, Lisa. Soon we were
joined by the rest of our party: my aunt Maryanne, the eldest of Fred
and Mary Trump's five children and a respected federal appeals court
judge; my uncle Robert, the baby of the family, who for a short time
had been one of Donald's employees in Atlantic City before leaving
on bad terms in the early 1990s, and his girlfriend; my aunt Elizabeth,
the middle Trump child, and her husband, Jim; my cousin David Desmond (Maryanne's only child and the oldest Trump grandchild) and
his wife; and a few of my aunts' closest friends. The only Trump sibling
who would be missing from the celebration was my father, Frederick
Crist Trump, Jr., the oldest son, whom everybody had called Freddy.
He had died more than thirty-five years before.

When we were finally all together, we checked in with the White
House security agents outside, then piled haphazardly into the two
White House vans like a JV lacrosse team. Some of the older guests
had trouble negotiating the steps. Nobody was comfortable squeezing
onto the bench seats. I wondered why the White House hadn't thought
to send at least one limo for my aunts.

As we pulled into the South Lawn driveway ten minutes later, two
guards came out of the security hut to inspect the underside of the van
before we drove through the front gate. After a short drive we stopped

at a small security building adjacent to the East Wing and disembarked. We went inside one by one as our names were called, handed over our phones and bags, and walked through a metal detector.

Once inside the White House, we walked in twos and threes through the long corridors, past windows looking out on gardens and lawns, past life-sized paintings of former first ladies. I stopped in front of Hillary Clinton's portrait and stood silently for a minute. I wondered again how this could have happened.

There was no reason for me ever to have imagined that I'd visit the White House, certainly not under these circumstances. The whole thing felt surreal. I looked around. The White House was elegant, grand, and stately, and I was about to see my uncle, the man who lived here, for the first time in eight years.

We emerged from the shadows of the hallway onto the portico surrounding the Rose Garden and stopped outside the Oval Office. Through the French doors, I could see that a meeting was still in progress. Vice President Mike Pence stood off to the side, but Speaker of the House Paul Ryan, Senator Chuck Schumer, and a dozen other congresspeople and staffers were gathered around Donald, who sat behind the Resolute Desk.

The tableau reminded me of one of my grandfather's tactics: he always made his supplicants come to him, either at his Brooklyn office or his house in Queens, and he remained seated while they stood. In late autumn 1985, a year after I had taken a leave of absence from Tufts University, I took my place in front of him and asked his permission to return to school. He looked up at me and said, "That's stupid. What do you want to do that for? Just go to trade school and become a receptionist."

"Because I want to get my degree." I must have said it with a hint of annoyance, because my grandfather narrowed his eyes and looked at me for a second as if reevaluating me. The corner of his mouth lifted in a sneer, and he laughed. "That's nasty," he said.

A few minutes later, the meeting broke up.

The Oval Office was both smaller and less intimate than I'd imagined. My cousin Eric and his wife, Lara, whom I'd never met, were standing right by the door, so I said, "Hi, Eric. It's your cousin Mary."

"Of course I know who you are," he said.

"Well, it's been a while," I said. "I think the last time we saw each other, you were still in high school."

He shrugged and said, "That's probably true." He and Lara walked away without his introducing us. I looked around. Melania, Ivanka, Jared, and Donny had arrived and were standing next to Donald, who remained seated. Mike Pence continued to lurk on the other side of the room with a half-dead smile on his face, like the chaperone everybody wanted to avoid.

I stared at him, hoping to make eye contact, but he never looked my way.

"Excuse me, everyone," the White House photographer, a petite young woman in a dark pantsuit, announced in an upbeat voice. "Let's get you all together so I can take some pictures before we go upstairs." She instructed us to surround Donald, who still had not gotten up from the desk.

The photographer raised her camera. "One, two, three, smile," she said.

After the pictures had been taken, Donald stood up and pointed to a framed black-and-white photograph of my grandfather, which was propped up on a table behind the desk. "Maryanne, isn't that a great picture of Dad?" It was the same photograph that had sat on the side table in the library of my grandparents' house. In it, my grandfather was still a young man, with receding dark hair, a mustache, and a look of command that I had never seen falter until his dementia set in. We'd all seen it thousands of times.

"Maybe you should have a picture of Mom, too," Maryanne suggested.

"That's a great idea," Donald said as though it had never occurred to him. "Somebody get me a picture of Mom."

We spent a few more minutes in the Oval Office, taking turns sitting behind the Resolute Desk. My brother took a picture of me, and when I looked at it later, I noticed my grandfather hovering behind me like a ghost.

The White House historian joined us just outside the Oval Office, and we proceeded to the Executive Residence on the second floor for a tour to be followed by dinner. Once upstairs, we proceeded to the Lincoln Bedroom. I took a quick look inside and was surprised to see a half-eaten apple on the bedside table. As the historian told us stories about what had happened in the room through the years, Donald pointed vaguely once in a while and declared, "This place has never looked better since George Washington lived here." The historian was too polite to point out that the house hadn't been opened until after Washington had died. The group moved down the hall toward the Treaty Room and the Executive Dining Room.

Donald stood in the doorway, greeting people as they entered. I was one of the last to arrive. I hadn't yet said hello, and when he saw me, he pointed at me with a surprised look on his face, then said, "I specifically asked for you to be here." That was the kind of thing he often said to charm people, and he had a knack for tailoring his comment to the occasion, which was all the more impressive because I knew it wasn't true. He opened his arms, and then, for the first time in my life, he hugged me.

The first thing I noticed about the Executive Dining Room was its beauty: the dark wood polished to perfection, the exquisite place settings, and the hand-drawn calligraphy on the place cards and menus (iceberg lettuce salad, mashed potatoes—Trump family staples—and Wagyu beef filet). The second thing I noticed after sitting down was the seating arrangement. In my family, you could always gauge your worth by where you were seated, but I didn't mind: all of the people I felt comfortable with—my brother and sister-in-law, Maryanne's stepdaughter and her husband—were seated near me.

Each of the waiters carried a bottle of red wine and a bottle of white.

Real wine, not TRUMP wine. That was unexpected. In my entire life, there had never been any alcohol at a family function. Only Coke and apple juice had been served at my grandparents' house.

Halfway through the meal, Jared walked into the dining room. "Oh, look," Ivanka said, clapping her hands, "Jared's back from his trip to the Middle East," as if we hadn't just seen him in the Oval Office. He walked over to his wife, gave her a quick kiss on the cheek, then bent over Donald, who was seated next to Ivanka. They spoke quietly for a couple of minutes. And then Jared left. He didn't acknowledge anybody else, not even my aunts. As he crossed the threshold, Donny leapt out of his chair and bounded after him like an excited puppy.

As dessert was being served, Robert stood up, wineglass in hand. "It is such an honor to be here with the president of the United States," he said. "Thank you, Mr. President, for allowing us to be here to celebrate our sisters' birthdays."

I thought back to the last time the family had celebrated Father's Day at Peter Luger Steak House in Brooklyn. Then, as now, Donald and Rob had been sitting next to each other with me directly across from them. Without any explanation, Donald had turned to Rob and said, "Look." He'd bared his teeth and pointed at his mouth.

"What?" Rob had asked.

Donald had simply pulled his lips back farther and pointed more emphatically.

Rob had started to look nervous. I had no idea what was going on but watched with amusement while I sipped my Coke.

"Look!" Donald had said through his gritted teeth. "What do you think?"

"What do you mean?" Rob's embarrassment was palpable. He had glanced around him to make sure nobody was looking at him and whispered, "Is there something in my teeth?" The bowls of creamed spinach scattered around the table rendered that a distinct possibility.

Donald had relaxed his mouth and stopped pointing. The contemptuous look on his face summed up the entire history of their relationship. "I got my teeth whitened. What do you think?" he had asked dryly.

After Rob's remarks, Donald shot him the same dismissive look I'd seen at Peter Luger's almost twenty years before. Then, Diet Coke glass in hand, Donald made some perfunctory remarks about my aunts' birthdays, after which he gestured toward his daughter-in-law. "Lara, there," he said. "I barely even knew who the fuck she was, honestly, but then she gave a great speech during the campaign in Georgia supporting me." By then, Lara and Eric had been together for almost eight years, so presumably Donald had at least met her at their wedding. But it sounded as if he hadn't known who she was until she had said something nice about him at a campaign rally during the election. As usual with Donald, the story mattered more than the truth, which was easily sacrificed, especially if a lie made the story sound better.

When Maryanne's turn came, she said, "I want to thank you for making the trip to celebrate our birthdays. We've come a long way since that night when Freddy dumped a bowl of mashed potatoes on Donald's head because he was being such a brat." Everybody familiar with the legendary mashed potato story laughed—everyone except Donald, who listened with his arms tightly crossed and a scowl on his face, as he did whenever Maryanne mentioned it. It upset him, as if he were that seven-year-old boy. He clearly still felt the sting of that long-ago humiliation.

Unprompted, my cousin Donny, who'd returned from chasing down Jared, stood up to speak. Instead of toasting our aunts, he gave a sort of campaign speech. "Last November, the American people saw something special and voted for a president who they knew understood them. They saw what a great family this is, and they connected with our values." I glanced at my brother and rolled my eyes.

I flagged down one of the waiters. "Can I have some more wine?" I asked.

He returned quickly with two bottles and asked if I preferred red or white.

"Yes, please," I said.

As soon as we finished dessert, everybody rose. Only two hours had elapsed since we'd entered the Oval Office, but the meal was over, and it was time to leave. From beginning to end we had spent about twice as much time at the White House as we ever had at my grandparents' house for Thanksgiving or Christmas but still less time with Donald than Kid Rock, Sarah Palin, and Ted Nugent would two weeks later.

Somebody suggested that we all take individual pictures with Donald (though not with the guests of honor). When it was my turn, Donald smiled for the camera and gave a thumbs-up, but I could see the exhaustion behind the smile. It seemed that keeping up the cheerful facade was wearing on him.

"Don't let them get you down," I said to him as my brother took the picture. It wasn't long after his first national security advisor had been fired in disgrace, and the cracks in his presidency were already beginning to show.

Donald jutted out his chin and clenched his teeth, looking for a moment like the ghost of my grandmother. "They're not going to get me," he said.

When Donald announced his run for the presidency on June 16, 2015, I didn't take it seriously. I didn't think *Donald* took it seriously. He simply wanted the free publicity for his brand. He'd done that sort of thing before. When his poll numbers started to rise and he may have received tacit assurances from Russian president Vladimir Putin that Russia would do everything it could to swing the election in his favor, the appeal of winning grew.

"He's a clown," my aunt Maryanne said during one of our regular lunches at the time. "This will never happen."

I agreed.

We talked about how his reputation as a faded reality star and failed businessman would doom his run. "Does anybody even believe the bullshit that he's a self-made man? What has he even accomplished on his own?" I asked.

"Well," Maryanne said, as dry as the Sahara, "he has had five bankruptcies."

When Donald started addressing the opioid crisis and using my father's history with alcoholism to burnish his anti-addiction bona fides to seem more sympathetic, both of us were angry.

"He's using your father's memory for political purposes," Maryanne said, "and that's a sin, especially since Freddy should have been the star of the family."

We thought the blatant racism on display during Donald's announcement speech would be a deal breaker, but we were disabused of that idea when Jerry Falwell, Jr., and other white evangelicals started endorsing him. Maryanne, a devout Catholic since her conversion five decades earlier, was incensed. "What the fuck is wrong with them?" she said. "The only time Donald went to church was when the cameras were there. It's mind boggling. He has no principles. None!"

Nothing Donald said during the campaign—from his disparagement of Secretary of State Hillary Clinton, arguably the most qualified presidential candidate in the history of the country, as a "nasty woman," to his mocking of Serge Kovaleski, a disabled *New York Times* reporter— deviated from my expectation of him. In fact, I was reminded of every family meal I'd ever attended during which Donald had talked about all of the women he considered ugly fat slobs or the men, usually more accomplished or powerful, he called losers while my grandfather and Maryanne, Elizabeth, and Robert all laughed and joined in. That kind of casual dehumanization of people was commonplace at the Trump dinner table. What *did* surprise me was that he kept getting away with it.

Then he received the nomination. The things I had thought would disqualify him seemed only to strengthen his appeal to his base. I still wasn't concerned—I was confident he could never be elected—but the idea that he had a shot at it was unnerving.

Late in the summer of 2016, I considered speaking out about the ways I knew Donald to be completely unqualified. By this time, he had emerged relatively unscathed from the Republican National Convention and his call for "Second Amendment people" to stop Hillary Clinton. Even his attack on Khizr and Ghazala Khan, Gold Star parents whose son Humayun, a US Army captain, had died in Iraq, seemed not to matter. When the majority of Republicans polled still supported him after the *Access Hollywood* tape was released, I knew I had made the right decision.

I began to feel as though I were watching my family history, and Donald's central role in it, playing out on a grand scale. Donald's competition in the race was being held to higher standards, just as my father had always been, while he continued to get away with—and even be rewarded for—increasingly crass, irresponsible, and despicable behavior. *This can't possibly be happening again*, I thought. But it was.

The media failed to notice that not one member of Donald's family, apart from his children, his son-in-law, and his current wife said a word in support of him during the entire campaign. Maryanne told me she was lucky because, as a federal judge, she needed to maintain her objectivity. She may have been the only person in the country, given her position as his sister and her professional reputation, who, if she had spoken out about Donald's complete unfitness for the office, might have made a difference. But she had her own secrets to keep, and I wasn't entirely surprised when she told me after the election that she'd voted for her brother out of "family loyalty."

Growing up in the Trump family, particularly as Freddy's child, presented certain challenges. In some ways I've been extremely fortunate. I attended excellent private schools and had the security of first-rate medical insurance for much of my life. There was also, though, a built-in sense of scarcity that applied to all of us, except Donald. After my grandfather died in 1999, I learned that my father's line had been erased from the will as if Fred Trump's oldest son had never existed, and a lawsuit followed. In the end, I concluded that if I spoke publicly about my uncle, I would be painted as a disgruntled, disinherited niece looking to cash in or settle a score.

In order to understand what brought Donald—and all of us—to this point, we need to start with my grandfather and his own need for recognition, a need that propelled him to encourage Donald's reckless hyperbole and unearned confidence that hid Donald's pathological weaknesses and insecurities.

As Donald grew up, he was forced to become his own cheerleader, first, because he needed his father to believe he was a better and more confident son than Freddy was; then because Fred required it of him; and finally because he began to believe his own hype, even as he paradoxically suspected on a very deep level that nobody else did. By the time of the election, Donald met any challenges to his sense of superiority with anger, his fear and vulnerabilities so effectively buried that he didn't even have to acknowledge they existed. And he never would.

In the 1970s, after my grandfather had already been preferring and promoting Donald for years, the New York media picked up the baton and began disseminating Donald's unsubstantiated hype. In the 1980s, the banks joined in when they began to fund his ventures. Their willingness (and then their need) to foster his increasingly unfounded claims to success hung on the hopes of recouping their losses.

After a decade during which Donald floundered, dragged down by bankruptcies and reduced to fronting for a series of failed products from steaks to vodka, the television producer Mark Burnett gave him yet another chance. *The Apprentice* traded on Donald's image as the brash, self-made dealmaker, a myth that had been the creation of my grandfather five decades earlier and that astonishingly, considering the vast trove of evidence disproving it, had survived into the new millennium almost entirely unaltered. By the time Donald announced his run for the Republican Party nomination in 2015, a significant percentage of the American population had been primed to believe that myth.

To this day, the lies, misrepresentations, and fabrications that are the sum total of who my uncle is are perpetuated by the Republican Party and white evangelical Christians. People who know better, such as Senate majority leader Mitch McConnell; true believers, such as Representative Kevin McCarthy, Secretary of State Mike Pompeo, and Attorney General William Barr; and others too numerous to name, have become, unwittingly or not, complicit in their perpetuation.

None of the Trump siblings emerged unscathed from my grandfather's sociopathy and my grandmother's illnesses, both physical and psychological, but my uncle Donald and my father, Freddy, suffered more than the rest. In order to get a complete picture of Donald, his psychopathologies, and the meaning of his dysfunctional behavior, we need a thorough family history.

In the last three years, I've watched as countless pundits, armchair psychologists, and journalists have kept missing the mark, using phrases such as "malignant narcissism" and "narcissistic personality disorder" in an attempt to make sense of Donald's often bizarre and self-defeating behavior. I have no problem calling Donald a narcissist—he meets all nine criteria as outlined in the *Diagnostic and Statistical Manual of Mental Disorders* (DSM-5)—but the label gets us only so far.

I received my PhD in clinical psychology from the Derner Institute of Advanced Psychological Studies, and while doing research for my dissertation I spent a year working on the admissions ward of Manhattan Psychiatric Center, a state facility, where we diagnosed, evaluated, and treated some of the sickest, most vulnerable patients. In addition to teaching graduate psychology, including courses in trauma, psychopathology, and developmental psychology, for several years as an adjunct professor, I provided therapy and psychological testing for patients at a community clinic specializing in addictions.

Those experiences showed me time and again that diagnosis doesn't exist in a vacuum. Does Donald have other symptoms we aren't aware of? Are there other disorders that might have as much or more explanatory power? Maybe. A case could be made that he also meets the criteria for antisocial personality disorder, which in its most severe form is generally considered sociopathy but can also refer to chronic criminality, arrogance, and disregard for the rights of others. Is there comorbidity? Probably. Donald may also meet some of the criteria for dependent personality disorder, the hallmarks of which include an inability to make decisions or take responsibility, discomfort with being alone, and going to excessive lengths to obtain support from others. Are there other factors that should be considered? Absolutely. He may have a long undiagnosed learning disability that for decades has interfered with his ability to process information. Also, he is alleged to drink upward of twelve Diet Cokes a day and sleep very little. Does he suffer from a substance- (in this case caffeine-) induced sleep disorder? He has a horrible diet and does not exercise, which may contribute to or exacerbate his other possible disorders.

The fact is, Donald's pathologies are so complex and his behaviors so often inexplicable that coming up with an accurate and comprehensive diagnosis would require a full battery of psychological and neuropsychological tests that he'll never sit for. At this point, we can't evaluate his day-to-day functioning because he is, in the West Wing, essentially institutionalized. Donald has been institutionalized for most of his adult life, so there is no way to know how he would thrive, or even survive, on his own in the real world.

At the end of my aunts' birthday party in 2017, as we lined up for our pictures, I could see that Donald was already under a kind of stress he'd never experienced before. As the pressures upon him have continued to mount over the course of the last three years, the disparity between the level of competence required for running a country and his incompetence has widened, revealing his delusions more starkly than ever before.

Many, but by no means all of us, have been shielded until now from the worst effects of his pathologies by a stable economy and a lack of serious crises. But the out-of-control COVID-19 pandemic, the possibility of an economic depression, deepening social divides along political lines thanks to Donald's penchant for division, and devastating uncertainty about our country's future have created a perfect storm of catastrophes that no one is less equipped than my uncle to manage. Doing so would require courage, strength of character, deference to experts, and the confidence to take responsibility and to course correct after admitting mistakes. His ability to control unfavorable situations by lying, spinning, and obfuscating has diminished to the point of impotence in the midst of the tragedies we are currently facing. His egregious and arguably intentional mishandling of the current catastrophe has led to a level of pushback and scrutiny that he's never experienced before, increasing his belligerence and need for petty revenge as he withholds vital funding, personal protective equipment, and ventilators that your tax dollars have paid for from states whose governors don't kiss his ass sufficiently.

In the 1994 film based on Mary Wollstonecraft Shelley's novel, Frankenstein's monster says, "I do know that for the sympathy of one living being, I would make peace with all. I have love in me the likes of which you can scarcely imagine and rage the likes of which you would not believe. If I cannot satisfy the one, I will indulge the other." After referencing that quote, Charles P. Pierce wrote in *Esquire*, "[Donald] doesn't plague himself with doubt about what he's creating around him. He is proud of his monster. He glories in its anger and its destruction and, while he cannot imagine its love, he believes with all his heart in its rage. He is Frankenstein without conscience."

That could more accurately have been said about Donald's father, Fred, with this crucial difference: Fred's monster—the only child of his who mattered to him—would ultimately be rendered unlovable by the very nature of Fred's preference for him. In the end, there would be no love for Donald at all, just his agonizing thirsting for it. The rage, left to grow, would come to overshadow everything else.

When Rhona Graff, Donald's longtime gatekeeper, sent me and my daughter an invitation to attend Donald's election-night party in New

York City, I declined. I wouldn't be able to contain my euphoria when Clinton's victory was announced, and I didn't want to be rude. At 5:00 the next morning, only a couple of hours after the opposite result had been announced, I was wandering around my house, as traumatized as many other people but in a more personal way: it felt as though 62,979,636 voters had chosen to turn this country into a macro version of my malignantly dysfunctional family.

Within a month of the election, I found myself compulsively watching the news and checking my Twitter feed, anxious and unable to concentrate on anything else. Though nothing Donald did surprised me, the speed and volume with which he started inflicting his worst impulses on the country—from lying about the crowd size at the inauguration and whining about how poorly he was treated to rolling back environmental protections, targeting the Affordable Care Act in order to take affordable health care away from millions of people, and enacting his racist Muslim ban—overwhelmed me. The smallest thing—seeing Donald's face or hearing my own name, both of which happened dozens of times a day—took me back to the time when my father had withered and died beneath the cruelty and contempt of my grandfather. I had lost him when he was only forty-two and I was sixteen. The horror of Donald's cruelty was being magnified by the fact that his acts were now official US policy, affecting millions of people.

The atmosphere of division my grandfather created in the Trump family is the water in which Donald has always swum, and division continues to benefit him at the expense of everybody else. It's wearing the country down, just as it did my father, changing us even as it leaves Donald unaltered. It's weakening our ability to be kind or believe in forgiveness, concepts that have never had any meaning for him. His administration and his party have become subsumed by his politics of grievance and entitlement. Worse, Donald, who understands nothing about history, constitutional principles, geopolitics, diplomacy (or anything else, really) and was never pressed to demonstrate such knowledge, has evaluated all of this country's alliances, and all of our social programs, solely through the prism of money, just as his father taught him to do. The costs and benefits of governing are considered in purely financial terms, as if the US Treasury were his personal piggy bank. To him, every dollar going out was his loss, while every dollar saved was his gain. In the midst of obscene plenty, one person, using all of the levers of power and taking every advantage at his disposal, would benefit himself and, conditionally, his immediate family, his cronies, and his sycophants; for the rest, there would never be enough to go around, which was exactly how my grandfather ran our family.

It's extraordinary that for all of the attention and coverage that Donald has received in the last fifty years, he's been subjected to very little scrutiny. Though his character flaws and aberrant behavior have been remarked upon and joked about, there's been very little effort to understand not only why he became who he is but how he's consistently failed up despite his glaring lack of fitness.

Donald has, in some sense, always been institutionalized, shielded from his limitations or his need to succeed on his own in the world. Honest work was never demanded of him, and no matter how badly he failed, he was rewarded in ways that are almost unfathomable. He continues to be protected from his own disasters in the White House, where a claque of loyalists applauds his every pronouncement or covers up his possible criminal negligence by normalizing it to the point that we've become almost numb to the accumulating transgressions. But now the stakes are far higher than they've ever been before; they are literally life and death. Unlike any previous time in his life, Donald's failings cannot be hidden or ignored because they threaten us all.

Although my aunts and uncles will think otherwise, I'm not writing this book to cash in or out of a desire for revenge. If either of those had been my intention, I would have written a book about our family years ago, when there was no way to anticipate that Donald would trade on his reputation as a serially bankrupt businessman and irrelevant reality show host to ascend to the White House; when it would have been safer because my uncle wasn't in a position to threaten and endanger whistleblowers and critics. The events of the last three years, however, have forced my hand, and I can no longer remain silent. By the time this book is published, hundreds of thousands of American lives will have been sacrificed on the altar of Donald's hubris and willful ignorance. If he is afforded a second term, it would be the end of American democracy.

No one knows how Donald came to be who he is better than his own family. Unfortunately, almost all of them remain silent out of loyalty or fear. I'm not hindered by either of those. In addition to the firsthand accounts I can give as my father's daughter and my uncle's only niece, I have the perspective of a trained clinical psychologist. *Too Much and Never Enough* is the story of the most visible and powerful family in the world. And I am the only Trump who is willing to tell it.

I hope this book will end the practice of referring to Donald's "strategies" or "agendas," as if he operates according to any organizing principles. He doesn't. Donald's ego has been and is a fragile and inadequate barrier between him and the real world, which, thanks to his father's money and power, he never had to negotiate by himself. Donald has always needed to perpetuate the fiction my grandfather started that he is strong, smart, and otherwise extraordinary, because facing the truth—that he is none of those things—is too terrifying for him to contemplate.

Donald, following the lead of my grandfather and with the complicity, silence, and inaction of his siblings, destroyed my father. I can't let him destroy my country.

PART ONE

The Cruelty Is the Point

CHAPTER ONE

The House

"Daddy, Mom's bleeding!"

They'd lived in the "House," as my grandparents' home was known, for less than a year, and it still felt unfamiliar, especially in the middle of the night, so when twelve-year-old Maryanne found her mother lying unconscious in one of the upstairs bathrooms—not the master bathroom but the bathroom she and her sister shared down the hall—she was already disoriented. There was blood all over the bathroom floor. Maryanne's terror was so great that it overcame her usual reluctance to disturb her father in his bedroom, and she flew to the other end of the house to rouse him.

Fred got out of bed, walked quickly down the hall, and found his wife unresponsive. With Maryanne at his heels, he rushed back to his bedroom, where there was a telephone extension, and placed a call.

Already a powerful man with connections at Jamaica Hospital, Fred was immediately put into touch with someone who could get an ambulance to the House and make sure the best doctors were waiting for them when they arrived at the emergency room. Fred explained the situation as best he could to the person on the other end. Maryanne heard him say "menstruation," an unfamiliar word that sounded strange coming out of her father's mouth.

Shortly after Mary arrived at the hospital, she underwent an emergency hysterectomy after doctors found that serious postpartum complications had gone undiagnosed after Robert's birth nine months earlier. The procedure led to an abdominal infection, and then further complications arose.

From what would become his usual spot by the telephone table in the library, Fred spoke briefly with one of Mary's doctors and, after hanging up the phone, called Maryanne to join him.

"They told me your mother won't make it through the night," he said to his daughter.

A little while later, as he was leaving for the hospital to be with his wife, he told her, "Go to school tomorrow. I'll call you if there's any change."

She understood the implication: I will call you if your mother dies.

Maryanne spent the night crying alone in her room while her younger siblings remained asleep in their beds, unaware of the calamity. She went to school the next day full of dread. Dr. James Dixon, the headmaster of Kew-Forest, a private school she had begun attending when her father joined the board of directors, came to get her from study hall. "There's a phone call for you in my office."

Maryanne was convinced that her mother was dead. The walk to the principal's office was like a walk to the scaffold. All the twelve-year-old could think was that she was going to be the acting mother of four children.

When she picked up the phone, her father simply said, "She's going to make it."

Mary would undergo two more surgeries over the next week, but she did indeed make it. Fred's pull at the hospital, which ensured that his wife got the very best doctors and care, had probably saved her life. But it would be a long road back to recovery.

For the next six months, Mary was into and out of the hospital. The long-term implications for her health were serious. She eventually developed severe osteoporosis from the sudden loss of estrogen that went with having her ovaries removed along with her uterus, a common but often unnecessary medical procedure performed at the time. As a result, she was often in excruciating pain from spontaneous fractures to her ever-thinning bones.

If we're lucky, we have, as infants and toddlers, at least one emotionally available parent who consistently fulfills our needs and responds to our desires for attention. Being held and comforted, having our feelings acknowledged and our upsets soothed are all critical for the healthy development of young children. This kind of attention creates a sense of safety and security that ultimately allows us to explore the world around us without excessive fear or unmanageable anxiety because we know we can count on the bedrock support of at least one caregiver.

Mirroring, the process through which an attuned parent reflects, processes, and then gives back to the baby the baby's own feelings, is another crucial part of a young child's development. Without mirroring, children are denied crucial information both about how their minds work and about how to understand the world. Just as a secure attachment to a primary caregiver can lead to higher levels of emotional intelligence, mirroring is the root of empathy.

Mary and Fred were problematic parents from the very beginning. My grandmother rarely spoke to me about her own parents or childhood, so I can only speculate, but she was the youngest of ten children—twenty-one years younger than her oldest sibling and four years younger than the second youngest—and she grew up in an often inhospitable environment in the early 1910s. Whether her own needs weren't sufficiently met when she was young or for some other reason, she was the kind of mother who used her children to comfort herself rather than comforting them. She attended to them when it was convenient for her, not when they needed her to. Often unstable and needy, prone to self-pity and flights of martyrdom, she frequently put herself first. Especially when it came to her sons, she acted as if there were nothing she could do for them.

During and after her surgeries, Mary's absence—both literal and emotional—created a void in the lives of her children. As hard as it must have been for Maryanne, Freddy, and Elizabeth, they were old enough to understand what was happening and could, to some extent, take care of themselves. The impact was especially dire for Donald and Robert, who at two and a half years and nine months old, respectively, were the most vulnerable of her children, especially since there was no one else to fill the void. The live-in housekeeper was undoubtedly overwhelmed by the sheer volume of housework. Their paternal grandmother, who lived nearby, prepared meals, but she was as terse and physically unaffectionate as her son. When Maryanne wasn't in school, much of the responsibility of taking care of the younger kids fell to her. (As a boy, Freddy wouldn't have been expected to help.) She gave them baths and got them ready for bed, but at twelve there was only so much she could do. The five kids were essentially motherless.

Whereas Mary was needy, Fred seemed to have no emotional needs at all. In fact, he was a high-functioning sociopath. Although uncommon, sociopathy is not rare, afflicting as much as 3 percent of the population. Seventy-five percent of those diagnosed are men. Symptoms of sociopathy include a lack of empathy, a facility for lying, an indifference to right and wrong, abusive behavior, and a lack of interest in the rights of others. Having a sociopath as a parent, especially if there is no one else around to mitigate the effects, all but guarantees severe disruption in how children understand themselves, regulate their emotions, and engage with the world. My grandmother was ill equipped to deal with the problems caused in her marriage by Fred's callousness, indifference, and controlling behaviors. Fred's lack of real human feeling, his rigidity as a parent and a husband, and his sexist belief in a woman's innate inferiority likely left her feeling unsupported.

Since Mary was emotionally and physically absent due to her injuries, Fred became, by default, the only available parent, but it would be a mistake to refer to him as a caregiver. He firmly believed that dealing with young children was not his job and kept to his twelve-hour-a-day, six-day-a-week job at Trump Management, as if his children could look after themselves. He focused on what was important to *him*: his increasingly successful business, which at the time was developing Shore Haven and Beach Haven, two massive residential projects in Brooklyn that were to date the most significant of his life.

Again, Donald and Robert in particular would have been in the most precarious position vis-à-vis Fred's lack of interest. All behavior exhibited by infants and toddlers is a form of attachment behavior, which seeks a positive, comforting response from the caregiver—a smile to elicit a smile, tears to prompt a hug. Even under normal circumstances, Fred would have considered any expressions of that kind an annoyance, but Donald and Robert were likely even needier because they missed their mother and were actively distressed by her absence. The greater their distress, however, the more Fred rebuffed them. He did not like to have demands made of him, and the annoyance provoked by his children's neediness set up a dangerous tension in the Trump household: by engaging in behaviors that were biologically designed to trigger soothing, comforting responses from their parents, the little boys instead provoked their father's anger or indifference when they were most vulnerable. For Donald and Robert, "needing" became equated with humiliation, despair, and hopelessness. Because Fred didn't want to be disturbed when he was home, it worked in his favor if his children learned one way or another not to need anything.

Fred's parenting style actually exacerbated the negative effects of Mary's absence. As a result of it, his children were isolated not just from the rest of the world but from one another. From then on it would become increasingly difficult for the siblings to find solidarity with other human beings, which is one of the reasons Freddy's brothers and sisters ultimately failed him; standing up for him, even helping him, would have risked their father's wrath.

When Mary became ill and Donald's main source of comfort and human connection was suddenly taken away from him, not only was there no one to help him make sense of it, Fred was the only person left that he could depend on. Donald's needs, which had been met inconsistently before his mother's illness, were barely met at all by his father. That Fred would, by default, become the primary source of Donald's solace when he was much more likely to be a source of fear or rejection put Donald into an intolerable position: being totally dependent on his father, who was also likely to be a source of his terror.

Child abuse is, in some sense, the experience of "too much" or "not enough." Donald directly experienced the "not enough" in the loss of connection to his mother at a crucial developmental stage, which was deeply traumatic. Without warning, his needs weren't being met, and his fears and longings went unsoothed. Having been abandoned by his mother for at least a year, and having his father fail not only to meet his needs but to make him feel safe or loved, valued or mirrored, Donald suffered deprivations that would scar him for life. The personality traits that resulted—displays of narcissism, bullying, grandiosity—finally made my grandfather take notice but not in a way that ameliorated any of the horror that had come before. As he grew older, Donald was subjected to my grandfather's "too-muchness" at second hand—witnessing what happened to Freddy when *he* was on the receiving end of too much attention, too much expectation, and, most saliently, too much humiliation.

From the beginning, Fred's self-interest skewed his priorities. His care of his children, such as it was, reflected his own needs, not theirs. Love meant nothing to him, and he could not empathize with their plight, one of the defining characteristics of a sociopath; he expected obedience, that was all. Children don't make such distinctions, and his kids believed that their father loved them or that they could somehow earn his love. But they also knew, if only on an unconscious level, that their father's "love," as they experienced it, was entirely conditional.

Maryanne, Elizabeth, and Robert, to greater or lesser degrees, experienced the same treatment as Donald because Fred wasn't interested in children at all. His oldest son and namesake received Fred's attention simply because he was being raised to carry on Fred's legacy.

In order to cope, Donald began to develop powerful but primitive defenses, marked by an increasing hostility to others and a seeming indifference to his mother's absence and father's neglect. The latter became a kind of learned helplessness over time because although it insulated him from the worst effects of his pain, it also made it extremely difficult (and in the long run I would argue impossible) for him to have any of his emotional needs met at all because he became too adept at acting as though he didn't have any. In place of those needs grew a kind of grievance and behaviors—including bullying, aggressiveness, and disrespect—that served their purpose in the moment but became more problematic over time. With appropriate care and attention, they might have been overcome. Unfortunately for Donald and everybody else on this planet, those behaviors became hardened into personality traits because once Fred started paying attention to his loud and difficult second son, he came to value them. Put another way, Fred Trump came to validate, encourage, and champion the things about Donald that rendered him essentially unlovable and that were in part the direct result of Fred's abuse.

Mary never completely recovered. Restless to begin with, she became an insomniac. The older kids would find her wandering around the House at all hours like a soundless wraith. Once Freddy found her standing at the top of a ladder painting the hallway in the middle of the night. In the morning her children sometimes found her unconscious in unexpected places; more than once, she ended up having to go to the hospital. That behavior became part of the life of the House. Mary got help for the physical injuries she sustained but none for whatever underlying psychological problems made her put herself into high-risk situations.

Beyond his wife's occasional injuries, Fred was aware of none of this and wouldn't have acknowledged the effects his particular brand of parenting had on his children then or later, even if he had recognized them. As far as he was concerned, he had been, for a brief time, faced with the limits of his wealth and power in fixing his wife's near-death health crisis. But ultimately Mary's medical challenges were a small blip in the grand scheme of things. Once she was on the mend and his Shore Haven and Beach Haven real estate developments, both phenomenal successes, were nearing completion, everything seemed once again to be going Fred's way.

When eight-year-old Freddy Trump asked why his very pregnant mother was getting so fat, talk at the dinner table ground to a halt. It was 1948, and the Trump family, which now consisted of four children—ten-year-old Maryanne, Freddy, five-year-old Elizabeth, and one-and-a-half-year-old Donald—were weeks away from moving into the twenty-three-room house that Fred was in the process of building. Mary looked down at her plate, and Fred's mother, also named Elizabeth, an almost daily visitor to the house, stopped eating.

Table etiquette at my grandparents' house was strict, and there were certain things Fred did not tolerate. "Keep your elbows off the table, this is not a horse's stable" was a frequent refrain, and Fred, knife in hand, would tap its handle against the forearm of any transgressor. (Rob and Donald took over that task when Fritz, David, and I were growing up, with a bit too much enthusiasm.) There were also things the children were not supposed to talk about, especially in front of their father or grandmother. When Freddy wanted to know how the baby had gotten there, Fred and his mother stood up as one, left the table without saying a word, and walked off. Fred wasn't a prude, but Elizabeth, a stern, formal woman who adhered to Victorian mores, very likely was.

Despite her own rigid views regarding gender roles, however, she had, many years earlier, made an exception for her son; a couple of years after Fred's father had died suddenly, Elizabeth had become her fifteen-year-old son's business partner.

That was made possible in part because her husband, Friedrich Trump, something of an entrepreneur, had left money and property valued at approximately $300,000 in today's currency.

Friedrich, born in Kallstadt, a small village in western Germany, left for the United States when he turned eighteen in 1885 in order to avoid mandatory military service. He eventually made the bulk of his money through ownership of restaurants and brothels in British Columbia. He lit out for the Yukon territories in time for the Gold Rush, cashing out just before the boom collapsed near the turn of the century.

In 1901, while visiting his family in Germany, Friedrich met and married Elizabeth Christ, a petite blond woman nearly twelve years his junior. He brought his new bride to New York, but one month after the birth of their first child, a girl they named Elizabeth, the couple returned to Germany with the intention of settling there permanently. Because of the circumstances under which Friedrich had originally left the country, he was told by authorities that he could not stay. Friedrich, his wife—now four months pregnant with their second child—and their two-year-old daughter returned for the last time to the United States in July 1905. Their two sons, Frederick and John, were born in 1905 and 1907, respectively. They eventually settled in Woodhaven, Queens, where all three children grew up speaking German.

When Friedrich died of the Spanish flu, twelve-year-old Fred became the man of the house. Despite the size of her husband's estate, Elizabeth found it difficult to make ends meet. The flu epidemic, which killed upward of 50 million people worldwide, had a destabilizing effect on what otherwise might have been a booming wartime economy. While still in high school, Fred took a series of odd jobs in order to help his mother financially and began to study the building trade. Becoming a builder had been his dream for as long as he could remember. He took every opportunity to learn the business, all aspects of which intrigued him, and during his sophomore year, with his mother's backing, he began building and selling garages in his neighborhood. He realized he was good at it, and from then on he had no other interests—none. Two years after Fred's high school graduation, Elizabeth created E. Trump and Son. She recognized her son's aptitude, and the business, which enabled her to handle financial transactions for her underage middle child—in the early twentieth century, people didn't attain legal majority until the age of twenty-one—was her way of supporting him. Both the business and the family thrived.

When Fred was twenty-five years old, he attended a dance where he met Mary Anne MacLeod, recently arrived from Scotland. According to family legend, when he returned home, he told his mother that he had met the girl he was going to marry.

Mary had been born the youngest of ten in 1912 in Tong, a village on the Isle of Lewis in the Outer Hebrides, located forty miles off the northwest coast of Scotland; her childhood had been bracketed by two global tragedies, the latter of which also deeply affected her future husband: World War I and the Spanish flu epidemic. Lewis had lost a disproportionate percentage of its male population during the war, and in a cruel twist of fate, two months after the armistice was signed in November 1918, a ship carrying soldiers home to the island from the mainland crashed into rocks just a few yards offshore in the early hours of January 1, 1919. More than 200 soldiers of the approximately 280 on board died in the brutally cold waters less than a mile from the safety of Stornoway Harbor. Much of the island's young adult male population was lost. Any young woman hoping to find a husband would have better luck elsewhere.

Mary, one of six daughters, was encouraged to journey to America, where the opportunities were greater and the men more plentiful.

In early May 1930, in a classic example of "chain migration," Mary boarded the RMS *Transylvania* in order to join two of her sisters who had already settled in the United States. Despite her status as a domestic servant, as a white Anglo-Saxon, Mary would have been allowed into the country even under her son's draconian new immigration rules introduced nearly ninety years later. She turned eighteen the day before her arrival in New York and met Fred not long after.

Fred and Mary were married on a Saturday in January 1936. After a reception at the Carlyle Hotel in Manhattan, they honeymooned in

Atlantic City for one night. On Monday morning, Fred was back at his Brooklyn office.

The couple moved into their first house on Wareham Road, just down the street from the house on Devonshire Road that Fred had shared with his mother. In those early years, Mary was still in awe of her head-spinning change in fortune, both financial and social. Instead of *being* the live-in help, she *had* live-in help; instead of competing for limited resources, she was the woman of the house. With free time to volunteer and money with which to shop, she never looked back, which perhaps explains why she was quick to judge others who came from similar circumstances. She and Fred put together an entirely conventional life with strictly drawn roles for husband and wife. He ran his business, which kept him in Brooklyn ten, sometimes twelve hours a day, six days a week. She ran the house, but he ruled it—and, at least in the beginning, so did his mother. Elizabeth was an intimidating mother-in-law who, during the first few years of her son's marriage, made sure that Mary understood who was really in charge: she wore white gloves when she visited, putting Mary on notice regarding the expectations she had for her daughter-in-law's housekeeping, which must have felt like a not-so-subtle mockery of her recent employment.

Despite Elizabeth's hazing, those early years were a time of great energy and possibility for Fred and Mary. Fred whistled his way down the stairs on his way to work, and when he returned home in the evening, he whistled his way up to his room, where he changed into a clean shirt before dinner.

Mary and Fred hadn't discussed baby names, so when their first child, a daughter, was born, they named her Maryanne, combining Mary's first and middle names. The couple's first son was born a year and a half later, on October 14, 1938, and named after his father—with one small change: Fred, Sr.'s, middle name was Christ, his mother's maiden name; his boy would be named Frederick Crist. Everybody except his father would call him Freddy.

It seems as though Fred mapped out his son's future before he was even born. Although he would feel the burdens of the expectations placed upon him when he grew older, Freddy benefited early on from his status in a way Maryanne and the other children would not. After all, he had a special place in his father's plans: he would be the means through which the Trump empire expanded and thrived in perpetuity.

Three and a half years passed before Mary gave birth to another child. Shortly before the arrival of Elizabeth, Fred left for an extended period to work in Virginia Beach. A housing shortage, the result of service members' returning from World War II, created an opportunity for him to build apartments for navy personnel and their families. Fred had had time to sharpen his skills and gain the reputation that got him the work because while other eligible men had enlisted, he had chosen not to serve, following in his father's footsteps.

Through his growing experience with building many houses simultaneously and his inherent skill at using local media to his own ends, Fred was introduced to well-connected politicians and learned through them how to call in favors at the right time, and, most important, chase government money. The lure in Virginia Beach, where Fred learned the advantage of building his real estate empire with government handouts, was the generous funding made available by the Federal Housing Administration (FHA). Founded in 1934 by President Franklin D. Roosevelt, the FHA seems to have strayed far from its original mandate by the time Fred began taking advantage of its largesse. Its chief purpose had been to ensure that enough affordable housing was being built for the country's constantly growing population. After World War II, the FHA seemed equally concerned with enriching developers such as Fred Trump.

The project in Virginia was also a chance to hone the expertise he'd begun to acquire in Brooklyn: building larger-scale projects as quickly, efficiently, and cheaply as possible while still managing to make them attractive to renters. When the commute back and forth to Queens became too inconvenient, Fred moved the entire family to Virginia Beach when Elizabeth was still an infant.

From Mary's perspective, other than finding herself in an unfamiliar environment, things were much the same in Virginia as they had been in Jamaica Estates. Fred worked long hours, leaving her alone with three children under the age of six. Their social life revolved around people he worked with or people whose services he needed. In 1944, when the FHA funding that had been financing Fred's projects dried up, the family returned to New York.

Once back in Jamaica Estates, Mary suffered a miscarriage, a serious medical event from which it took her months to recover fully. Doctors warned her against further pregnancies, but Mary found herself expecting again a year later. The miscarriage created large age gaps between the older and younger children, with Elizabeth floating in the middle, almost four years younger or older than her two closest siblings. Maryanne and Freddy were so much older than the youngest children that it was almost as if they belonged to two different generations.

Donald, the couple's fourth child and second son, was born in 1946, just as Fred began plans for the new family house. He purchased a half-acre lot directly behind the Wareham Road house situated on a hill overlooking Midland Parkway, a wide tree-lined thoroughfare that runs through the entire neighborhood. When the kids found out about the impending move, they joked that they didn't need to hire a moving truck; they could just roll their belongings down the hill.

At more than four thousand square feet, the House was the most impressive residence on the block but still smaller and less grand than many of the mansions that dominated the hills in the northern part of the neighborhood. Set at the top of a rise, the House cast shadows in the afternoon over the wide flagstone steps that led from the sidewalk to the front door, an entrance we used only on special occasions. The lawn jockeys, racist reminders of the Jim Crow era, were first painted pink and then replaced with flowers. The faux coat of arms on the pediment over the front door remained.

Although Queens would eventually be one of the most diverse places on the planet, in the 1940s, when my grandfather bought the land and built the imposing redbrick Georgian colonial with the twenty-foot columns, the borough was 95 percent white. The upper-middle-class neighborhood of Jamaica Estates was even whiter. When the first Italian American family moved to the neighborhood in the 1950s, Fred was scandalized.

In 1947, Fred embarked on the most important large-scale project of his career up until that point: Shore Haven, a proposed complex in Bensonhurst, Brooklyn, comprising thirty-two six-story buildings and a shopping center spread over more than thirty acres. The draw this time was the $9 million in FHA funds that would be paid to Fred directly, just as Donald would later capitalize on tax breaks lavished on him by both the city and the state. Fred had previously described the type of people renting the 2,201 apartments as "unwholesome," the implication being that upstanding people lived only in the single-family dwellings that had been his early specialty. But $9 million can be very persuasive. Around that time, when it became clear that Fred's fortune would only continue to grow, he and his mother set up trust funds for his children that would shield the money from taxation.

Though an iron-fisted autocrat at home and in his office, Fred had become expert at gaining access to and kowtowing to more powerful and better-connected men. I don't know how he acquired the skill, but he would later pass it on to Donald. Over time, he developed ties to leaders of the Brooklyn Democratic Party, the New York State political machine, and the federal government, many of whom were major players in the real estate industry. If getting funding meant sucking up to the local politicos who held the FHA purse strings, so be it. He joined an exclusive beach club on the south shore of Long Island and later North Hills Country Club, both of which he considered excellent places to entertain, impress, and rub elbows with the men best positioned to funnel government funds his way, much as Donald would do at Le Club in New York in the 1970s and at golf clubs everywhere.

As Donald was later alleged to do with Trump Tower and his casinos in Atlantic City, Fred was said to have worked discreetly with the Mob in order to keep the peace. When he got the green light for another development—Beach Haven, a forty-acre, twenty-three-building complex in Coney Island that would net him $16 million in FHA funding—it was clear that his strategy of building on the taxpayer's dime was a winner.

Though Fred's business was built on the back of government financing, he loathed paying taxes and would do anything to avoid doing so. At the height of his empire's expansions, he never spent a dime he didn't have to, and he *never* acquired debt, an imperative that did not extend to his sons. Bound by the scarcity mentality that had been shaped by World War I and the Depression, Fred owned his properties free and clear. The profits his company generated from rents were enormous. In relation to his net worth, Fred, whose children said he was "tighter than a duck's ass," lived a relatively modest life. Despite the piano lessons and private summer camps—of a piece with his notion of what was expected for a man of his station in life—his two oldest children grew up feeling "white poor." Maryanne and Freddy walked the fifteen minutes to Public School 131, and when they wanted to go into the city, as everyone in the outer boroughs of New York refers to Manhattan, they took the subway from 169th Street. Of course, they weren't poor—and aside from some early struggles after his father's death, Fred never had been, either.

Fred's wealth afforded him the opportunity to live anywhere, but he would spend most of his adult life less than twenty minutes from where he had grown up. With the exception of a few weekends in Cuba with Mary in the early days of their marriage, he never left the country. After he completed the project in Virginia, he rarely even left New York City.

His business empire, though large and lucrative, was equally provincial. The number of buildings he came to own exceeded four dozen, but the buildings themselves had relatively few floors and were uniformly utilitarian. His holdings remained almost exclusively in Brooklyn and Queens. The glitz, glamour, and diversity of Manhattan might as well have been on another continent as far as he was concerned, and in those early years, it seemed just as far out of reach.

By the time the family moved into the House, everybody in the neighborhood knew who Fred Trump was, and Mary embraced her role as the wife of a rich, influential businessman. She became heavily involved in charity work, including at the Women's Auxiliary at Jamaica Hospital and the Jamaica Day Nursery, chairing luncheons and attending black-tie fund-raisers.

No matter how great the couple's success, there remained for both Fred and Mary a tension between their aspirations and their instincts. In Mary's case it was likely the result of a childhood marked by scarcity if not outright deprivation and in Fred's a caution deriving from the massive loss of life, including his father's, during the Spanish flu and World War I, as well as the economic uncertainty his family had experienced after his father's death. Despite the millions of dollars pouring in from Trump Management every year, Fred still couldn't resist picking up unused nails or reverse engineering a cheaper pesticide. Despite the ease with which Mary took to her new status and the perks that went along with it, including a live-in housekeeper, she spent most of her time in the House, sewing, cooking, and doing laundry. It was as if neither of them could quite figure out how to reconcile what they could possibly have and what they would actually allow themselves.

Although frugal, Fred was neither modest nor humble. Early in his career, he had lied about his age in order to appear more precocious. He had had a propensity for showmanship, and he often trafficked in hyperbole—everything was "great," "fantastic," and "perfect." He inundated local newspapers with press releases about his newly completed homes and gave numerous interviews extolling the virtues of his properties. He plastered south Brooklyn with ads and hired a barge covered with ads to float just off the shoreline. But he wasn't nearly as good at it as Donald would come to be. He could handle interacting one on one and currying favor with his politically connected betters, but speaking in front of large groups or navigating television interviews was beyond him. He took a Dale Carnegie public speaking course, but he was so bad at it that even his usually obedient children teased him about it. Just as some people have a face for radio, Fred had a level of social confidence made for back rooms and print media. That fact would figure significantly in his later support of his second son at the expense of his first.

When Fred heard about Norman Vincent Peale in the 1950s, Peale's shallow message of self-sufficiency appealed to him enormously. The pastor of Marble Collegiate Church in midtown Manhattan, Peale was very fond of successful businessmen. "Being a merchant isn't getting money," he wrote. "Being a merchant is serving the people." Peale was a charlatan, but he was a charlatan who headed up a rich and powerful church, and he had a message to sell. Fred wasn't a reader, but it was impossible not to know about Peale's wildly popular bestseller, *The Power of Positive Thinking*. The title alone was enough for Fred, and he decided to join Marble Collegiate although he and his family rarely attended.

Fred already had a positive attitude and unbounded faith in himself. Although he could be serious and formal, or dismissive to people such as his children's friends, who were of no interest to him, he smiled easily, even when he was telling somebody he or she was nasty, and was usually in a good mood. He had reason to be; he was in control of everything in his world. With the exception of his father's death, the course of his life had been fairly smooth and full of supportive family and colleagues. Since his early days building garages, his success had been on an almost constantly upward trajectory. He worked hard, but unlike most people who work hard, he was rewarded with government grants, the almost limitless help of highly connected cronies, and immensely good fortune. Fred didn't need to read *The Power of Positive Thinking* in order to co-opt, for his own purposes, the most superficial and self-serving aspects of Peale's message.

Anticipating the prosperity gospel, Peale's doctrine proclaimed that you need only self-confidence in order to prosper in the way God wants you to. "[O]bstacles are simply not permitted to destroy your happiness and well-being. You need be defeated only if you are willing to be," Peale wrote. That view neatly confirmed what Fred already thought: he was rich because he deserved to be. "Believe in yourself! Have faith in your abilities! . . . A sense of inferiority and inadequacy interferes with the attainment of your hopes, but self-confidence leads to self-realization and successful achievement." Self-doubt wasn't part of Fred's makeup, and he never considered the possibility of his own defeat. As Peale also wrote, "It is appalling to realize the number of pathetic people who are hampered and made miserable by the malady popularly called the inferiority complex."

Peale's proto–prosperity gospel actually complemented the scarcity mentality Fred continued to cling to. For him, it was not "the more you have, the more you can give." It was "the more you have, the more you have." Financial worth was the same as self-worth, monetary value was human value. The more Fred Trump had, the better he was. If he gave something to someone else, that person would be worth more and he less. He would pass that attitude on to Donald in spades.

CHAPTER TWO

The First Son

Freddy's status as the oldest son in the family had gone from protecting him from Fred's worst impulses as a parent to being an immense and stressful burden. As he got older, he became torn between the responsibility that his father had placed on him and his natural inclination to live life his own way. Fred wasn't torn at all: his son should be spending time at the Trump Management office on Avenue Z, not with his friends out on Peconic Bay, where he learned to love boating, fishing, and waterskiing. By the time Freddy was a teenager, he knew what his future held and he knew what his father expected of him. He also knew that he wasn't measuring up. His friends noticed that their usually laid-back and fun-loving friend became anxious and self-conscious around Fred, whom Freddy and his friends called "the Old Man." Solidly built and standing six feet one, Fred was an imposing figure with hair slicked back from a receding hairline who rarely wore anything but a well-tailored three-piece suit. He was stiff and formal around kids, he never played ball or games of any kind with them, and it seemed as if he had never been young.

If the boys were tossing a ball around in the basement, the sound of the garage door opening was enough to cause Freddy to freeze. "Stop! My dad's home." When Fred came into the room, the boys had the impulse to stand and salute him.

"So what's this?" he'd ask as he shook each boy's hand.

"Nothing, Dad," Freddy would say. "Everybody's getting ready to leave soon."

Freddy remained quiet and on high alert as long as the Old Man was home.

In his early teens, Freddy started lying to his father about his life outside the House to avoid the mockery or disapproval he knew the truth would bring down on him. He lied about what he and friends got up to after school. He lied about smoking—a habit Maryanne had introduced him to when he was twelve and she was thirteen—telling his father that he was going around the corner to help his best friend, Billy Drake, walk a nonexistent dog. Fred, for instance, wasn't going to find out that Freddy and his buddy Homer from St. Paul's School had stolen a hearse for a joyride. Before returning the vehicle to the funeral home, Freddy pulled into a gas station to fill up the tank. As he got out of the car and walked toward the pump, Homer, who was lying down in the back to see what it was like, sat up. A man at the pump across from them, thinking he'd just seen a corpse rising from the dead, screamed, and Freddy and Homer laughed until they cried. Freddy lived for that kind of prank, but he regaled his brothers and sisters with his exploits only if their father wasn't home.

For some of the Trump kids, lying was a way of life, and for Fred's oldest son, lying was defensive—not simply a way to circumvent his father's disapproval or to avoid punishment, as it was for the others, but a way to survive. Maryanne, for instance, never went against her father, perhaps out of fear of an ordinary punishment such as being grounded or sent to her room. For Donald, lying was primarily a mode of self-aggrandizement meant to convince other people he was better than he actually was. For Freddy, the consequences of going against his father were different not only in degree but in kind, so lying became his only defense against his father's attempts to suppress his natural sense of humor, sense of adventure, and sensitivity.

Peale's ideas about inferiority complexes helped shape Fred's harsh judgments about Freddy, while also allowing him to evade taking responsibility for any of his children. Weakness was perhaps the greatest sin of all, and Fred worried that Freddy was more like his own brother, John, the MIT professor: soft and, though not unambitious, interested in the wrong things, such as engineering and physics, which Fred found esoteric and unimportant. Such softness was unthinkable in his namesake, and by the time the family had moved into the House when Freddy was ten, Fred had already determined to toughen him up. Like most people who aren't paying attention to where they're going, however, he overcorrected.

"That's stupid," Fred said whenever Freddy expressed a desire to get a pet or played a practical joke. "What do you want to do that for?" Fred said with such contempt in his voice that it made Freddy flinch, which only annoyed Fred more. Fred hated it when his oldest son screwed up or failed to intuit what was required of him, but he hated it even more when, after being taken to task, Freddy apologized. "Sorry, Dad," Fred would mock him. Fred wanted his oldest son to be a "killer" in his parlance (for what reason it's impossible to say—collecting rent in Coney Island wasn't exactly a high-risk endeavor in the 1950s), and he was temperamentally the opposite of that.

Being a killer was really code for being invulnerable. Although Fred didn't seem to feel anything about his father's death, the suddenness of it had taken him by surprise and knocked him off balance. Years later, when discussing it, he said, "Then he died. Just like that. It just didn't seem real. I wasn't that upset. You know how kids are. But I got upset watching my mother crying and being so sad. It was seeing her that made me feel bad, not my own feelings about what had happened."

The loss, in other words, had made him feel vulnerable, not because of his own feelings but because of his mother's feelings, which he likely felt were being imposed on him, especially as he did not share them. That imposition must have been very painful. In that moment, he wasn't the center of the universe, and that was unacceptable. Going forward, he refused to acknowledge or feel loss. (I never heard him or anyone else in my family speak about my great-grandfather.) As far as Fred was concerned, he was able to move on because nothing particularly important *had* been lost.

Subscribing as Fred did to Norman Vincent Peale's ideas about human failings, he didn't grasp that by ridiculing and questioning Freddy, he was creating a situation in which low self-esteem was almost inevitable. Fred was simultaneously telling his son that he had to be an unqualified success and that he never could be. So Freddy existed in a system that was all punishment, no reward. The other children, especially Donald, couldn't have helped but notice.

The situation was somewhat different for Donald. With the benefit of a seven-and-a-half-year age difference, he had plenty of time to learn from watching Fred humiliate his older brother and Freddy's resulting shame. The lesson he learned, at its simplest, was that it was wrong to be like Freddy: Fred didn't respect his oldest son, so neither would Donald. Fred thought Freddy was weak, and therefore so did Donald. It would take a long time before the two brothers, in very different ways, came to adapt themselves to the truth of this.

It's difficult to understand what goes on in any family—perhaps hardest of all for the people in it. Regardless of how a parent treats a child, it's almost impossible for that child to believe that parent means them any harm. It was easier for Freddy to think that his father had his son's best interests at heart and that he, Freddy, was the problem. In other words, protecting his love for his father was more important than protecting himself from his father's abuse. Donald would have taken his father's treatment of his brother at face value: "Dad's not trying to hurt Freddy. He's only trying to teach us how to be real men. And Freddy's failing."

Abuse can be quiet and insidious just as often as, or even more often than, it is loud and violent. As far as I know, my grandfather wasn't a physically violent man or even a particularly angry one. He didn't have to be; he expected to get what he wanted and almost always did. It wasn't his inability to fix his oldest son that infuriated him, it was the fact that Freddy simply wasn't what he wanted him to be. Fred dismantled his oldest son by devaluing and degrading every aspect of his personality and his natural abilities until all that was left was self-recrimination and a desperate need to please a man who had no use for him.

The only reason Donald escaped the same fate is that his personality served his father's purpose. That's what sociopaths do: they co-opt others and use them toward their own ends—ruthlessly and efficiently, with no tolerance for dissent or resistance. Fred destroyed Donald, too, but not by snuffing him out as he did Freddy; instead, he short-circuited Donald's ability to develop and experience the entire spectrum of human emotion. By limiting Donald's access to his own feelings and rendering many of them unacceptable, Fred perverted his son's perception of the world and damaged his ability to live in it. His capacity to be his own person, rather than an extension of his father's ambitions, became severely limited. The implications of that limitation became clearer when Donald entered school. Neither of his parents had interacted with him in a way that helped him make sense of his world, which contributed to his inability to get along with other people and remained a constant buffer between him and his siblings. It also made reading social cues extremely difficult, if not impossible, for him—a problem he has to this day.

Ideally, the rules at home reflect the rules of society, so when children go out into the world, they generally know how to behave. When kids go to school, they're supposed to know that they shouldn't take other children's toys and they're not supposed to hit or tease other children. Donald didn't understand any of that because the rules in the House, at least as they applied to the boys—be tough at all costs, lying is okay, admitting you're wrong or apologizing is weakness—clashed with the rules he encountered at school. Fred's fundamental beliefs about how the world worked—in life, there can be only one winner and everybody else is a loser (an idea that essentially precluded the ability to share) and kindness is weakness—were clear. Donald knew, because he had seen it with Freddy, that failure to comply with his father's rules was punished by severe and often public humiliation, so he continued to adhere to them even outside his father's purview. Not surprisingly, his understanding of "right" and "wrong" would clash with the lessons taught in most elementary schools.

Donald's growing arrogance, in part a defense against his feelings of abandonment and an antidote to his lack of self-esteem, served as a protective cover for his deepening insecurities. As a result, he was able to keep most people at arm's length. It was easier for him that way. Life in the House made all the children in one way or another uncomfortable with emotions—either expressing them or being confronted with them. It was probably worse for the boys, for whom the acceptable range of human feeling was extremely narrow. (I never saw any man in my family cry or express affection for one another in any way other than the handshake that opened and closed any encounter.) Getting close to other children or authority figures may have felt like a dangerous betrayal of his father. Nonetheless, Donald's displays of confidence, his belief that society's rules didn't apply to him, and his exaggerated display of self-worth drew some people to him. A large minority of people still confuse his arrogance for strength, his false bravado for accomplishment, and his superficial interest in them for charisma.

Donald had discovered early on how easy it was to get under Robert's pale skin and push him past his limits; it was a game he never tired of playing. Nobody else would have bothered—Robert was so skinny and quiet that there was no sport in tormenting him—but Donald enjoyed flexing his power, even if only over his younger, smaller, and even thinner-skinned brother. Once, out of frustration and helplessness, Robert kicked a hole in their bathroom door, which got him into trouble despite the fact that Donald had driven him to it. When his mother told Donald to stop, he didn't; when Maryanne and Freddy told him to stop, he didn't.

One Christmas the boys received three Tonka trucks, which soon became Robert's favorite toys. As soon as Donald figured that out, he started hiding them from his little brother and pretending he had no idea where they were. The last time it happened, when Robert's tantrum spiraled out of control, Donald threatened to dismantle the trucks in front of him if he didn't stop crying. Desperate to save them, Robert ran to his mother. Mary's solution was to hide the trucks in the attic, effectively punishing Robert, who'd done nothing wrong, and leaving Donald feeling invincible. He wasn't yet being rewarded for selfishness, obstinacy, or cruelty, but he wasn't being punished for those flaws, either.

Mary remained a bystander. She didn't intervene in the moment and didn't comfort her son, acting as if it weren't her place to do so. Even for the 1950s, the family was split deeply along gender lines. Despite the fact that Fred's mother had been his partner—she had literally started his business—it's clear that Fred and his wife were never partners. The girls were her purview, the boys his. When Mary made her annual trip home to the Isle of Lewis, only Maryanne and Elizabeth accompanied her. Mary cooked the boys' meals and laundered their clothes but didn't feel that it was her place to guide them. She rarely interacted with the boys' friends, and her relationships with her sons, already marred by their early experiences with her, became increasingly distant.

When Freddy, at fourteen, dumped a bowl of mashed potatoes on his then-seven-year-old brother's head, it wounded Donald's pride so deeply that he'd still be bothered by it when Maryanne brought it up in her toast at the White House birthday dinner in 2017. The incident wasn't a big deal—or it shouldn't have been. Donald had been tormenting Robert, again, and nobody could get him to stop. Even at seven, he felt no need to listen to his mother, who, having failed to heal the rift between them after her illness, he treated with contempt. Finally, Robert's crying and Donald's needling became too much, and in a moment of improvised expedience that would become family legend, Freddy picked up the first thing at hand that wouldn't cause any real damage: the bowl of mashed potatoes.

Everybody laughed, and they couldn't stop laughing. And they were laughing *at* Donald. It was the first time Donald had been humiliated by someone he even then believed to be beneath him. He hadn't understood that humiliation was a weapon that could be wielded by only one person in a fight. That Freddy, of all people, could drag him into a world where humiliation could happen to *him* made it so much worse. From then on, he would never allow himself to feel that feeling again. From then on, he would wield the weapon, never be at the sharp end of it.

Chapter Three

The Great I-Am

B y the time Maryanne left for Mount Holyoke and, a couple of years later, Freddy for Lehigh University, Donald had already had plenty of experience watching his older brother struggle with, and largely fail to meet, their father's expectations. They were vague, of course. Fred had the authoritarian's habit of assuming that his underlings knew what to do without being told. Generally, the only way to know if you were doing something right was if you didn't get dressed down for it.

But it was one thing for Donald to stay out of his father's crosshairs and another to get into his good graces. Toward that end, Donald all but eradicated any qualities he might have shared with his older brother. Except for the occasional fishing trip with Freddy and his friends, Donald would become a creature of country clubs and offices, golf being the only thing on which he and his father differed. He would also double down on the behaviors he had thus far gotten away with: bullying, pointing the finger, refusing to take responsibility, and disregarding authority. He says that he "pushed back" against his father and Fred "respected" that. The truth is, he was able to push back against his father because Fred let him. When he was very young, Fred's attention was not trained on him; his focus was elsewhere—on his business and his oldest son, that's it. Eventually, when Donald went away to military school at thirteen, Fred began to admire Donald's disregard of authority. Although a strict parent in general, Fred accepted Donald's arrogance and bullying—after he actually started to notice them—because he identified with the impulses.

Encouraged by his father, Donald eventually started to believe his own hype. By the time he was twelve, the right side of his mouth was curled up in an almost perpetual sneer of self-conscious superiority, and Freddy had dubbed him "the Great I-Am," echoing a passage from Exodus he'd learned in Sunday school in which God first reveals himself to Moses.

Because of the disastrous circumstances in which he was raised, Donald knew intuitively, based on plenty of experience, that he would never be comforted or soothed, especially when he most needed to be. There was no point, then, in acting needy. And whether he knew it on any level or not, neither of his parents was ever going to see him for who he truly was or might have been—Mary was too depleted and Fred was interested only in whichever of his sons could be of most use—so he became whatever was most expedient. The rigid personality he developed as a result was a suit of armor that often protected him against pain and loss. But it also kept him from figuring out how to trust people enough to get close to them.

Freddy was terrified to ask Fred for anything. Donald had seen the results of that reticence. Whenever Freddy deviated even slightly from Fred's often unspoken expectations, he ended up humiliated or shamed. Donald would try something different: he chose instead to ingratiate himself with their father by smashing through every barrier his older brother never dared test. He knew exactly how to play it: when Freddy flinched, Donald shrugged. He took what he wanted without asking for permission not because he was brave but because he was afraid not to. Whether Donald understood the underlying message or not, Fred did: in family, as in life, there could be only one winner; everybody else had to lose. Freddy kept trying and failing to do the right thing; Donald began to realize that there was nothing he could do wrong, so he stopped trying to do anything "right." He became bolder and more aggressive because he was rarely challenged or held to account by the only person in the world who mattered—his father. Fred liked his killer attitude, even if it manifested as bad behavior.

Every one of Donald's transgressions became an audition for his father's favor, as if he were saying "See, Dad, I'm the tough one. I'm the killer." He kept piling on because there wasn't any resistance—until there was. But it didn't come from his father.

Though Donald's behavior didn't bother Fred—given his long hours at the office, he wasn't often around to witness much of what happened at home—it drove his mother to distraction. Mary couldn't control him at all, and Donald disobeyed her at every turn. Any attempt at discipline by her was rebuffed. He talked back. He couldn't ever admit he was wrong; he contradicted her even when she was right; and he refused to back down. He tormented his little brother and stole his toys. He refused to do his chores or anything else he was told to do. Perhaps worst of all to a fastidious woman like her, he was a slob who refused to pick up after himself no matter how much she threatened him. "Wait until your father comes home" had been an effective threat with Freddy, but to Donald it was a joke that his father seemed to be in on.

Finally, by 1959, Donald's misbehavior—fighting, bullying, arguing with teachers—had gone too far. Kew-Forest had reached its limits. Fred's being on the school's board of trustees cut two ways: on the one hand, Donald's behavior had been overlooked longer than it otherwise might have; on the other, it caused Fred some inconvenience. Name-calling and teasing kids too young to fight back had escalated into physical altercations. Fred didn't mind Donald's acting out, but it had become intrusive and time consuming for him. When one of his fellow board members at Kew-Forest recommended sending Donald to New York Military Academy as a way to rein him in, Fred went along with it. Throwing him in with military instructors and upperclassmen who wouldn't put up with his shit might toughen up Fred's burgeoning protégé even more. Fred had more important things to do than deal with Donald.

I don't know if Mary had any say in the final decision, but she didn't fight for her son to stay home, either, a failure Donald couldn't help but notice. It must have felt like a replay of all the times she'd abandoned him in the past.

Over Donald's objections, he was enrolled at NYMA, a private boys' boarding school sixty miles north of New York City. The other kids in the family referred to NYMA as a "reform school"—it wasn't prestigious like St. Paul's, which Freddy had attended. Nobody sent their sons to NYMA for a better education, and Donald understood it rightly as a punishment.

When Freddy found out, he told his friends with some bewilderment, "Yeah, they can't control him." It didn't really make any sense. His father always seemed to be in control of *everybody*. What Freddy didn't understand was that their father wasn't interested in Donald the same way he was interested in him. If Fred had tried to discipline Donald, he would have been disciplined, but before Donald was sent away, Fred just wasn't interested enough to bother with Donald or the other three children.

Parents always have different effects on their children, no matter the dynamics of the family, but for the Trump children, the effects of Fred and Mary's particular pathologies on their offspring were extreme. As the five, at different times and in different ways, got ready to go out in the world, their disadvantages were already apparent:

Maryanne, the firstborn, was saddled with being a smart, ambitious girl in a misogynistic family. She was the oldest, but because she was a girl, Freddy, the oldest boy, got all of her father's attention. She was left to align herself with her mother, who had no power in the house. As a result, after having her heart broken when she was rejected by the Dartmouth home economics program, she settled for Mount Holyoke College, a "virtual nunnery," as she put it. Ultimately, she did what she believed she was supposed to do because she thought her father cared.

Freddy's problem was his failure to be a different person entirely.

Elizabeth's problem was her family's indifference. She was not just the middle child (and a girl) but separated by her brothers on either side by an age gap of three or four years. Shy and timid as an adolescent, she didn't speak much, having learned the lesson that neither of her parents was really listening. Still she remained devoted to them until well into middle age, returning to the House every weekend, still hoping for "Poppy's" attention.

Donald's problem was that the combative, rigid persona he developed in order to shield him from the terror of his early abandonment, along with his having been made to witness his father's abuse of Freddy, cut him off from real human connection.

Robert's problem was that he was the youngest, an afterthought.

Nothing Maryanne, Elizabeth, or Robert did would gain Fred's approval; they were of no interest to him. Like planets orbiting a particularly large sun, the five of them were kept apart by the force of his will, even as they moved along the paths he set for them.

Freddy's plans for the future still entailed becoming his father's right-hand man at Trump Management, but the first time Freddy took off from the airstrip of the Slatington Flying Club behind the controls of a Cessna 170 in 1961, his perspective shifted.

As long as he fulfilled the requirements of his business major and kept his grades up, he could fly, pledge a fraternity, and join the US Air Force Reserve Officer Training Corps (ROTC). On a lark, Freddy chose Sigma Alpha Mu, a historically Jewish fraternity. Whether it was a conscious rebuke of his father, who frequently used phrases such as "Jew me down," Freddy's fraternity brothers eventually became some of his best friends. Joining ROTC served another purpose entirely. Freddy craved discipline that made sense. He thrived in ROTC's transparent system of achievement and reward. If you did what you were told, your obedience was recognized. If you met or exceeded expectations, you were rewarded. If you made a mistake or failed to follow an order, you received discipline that was commensurate with the infraction. He loved the hierarchy; he loved the uniforms; he loved the medals that were clear symbols of accomplishment. When you are wearing a uniform, other people can easily identify who you are and what you've accomplished, and you are acknowledged accordingly. It was the opposite of life with Fred Trump, by whom good work was expected but never acknowledged; only mistakes were called out and punished.

Getting his pilot's license made sense in the same way ROTC did: you log a certain number of hours, you get certified on particular instruments, you get a license. His flying lessons eventually became his number one priority. Just as with boating, he took flying very seriously and began skipping card games with his fraternity brothers to study or log another hour at the flight school. But it wasn't just the pleasure of finding something he excelled at, it was the joy of total freedom, which he'd never before experienced.

In the summer, Freddy worked for Fred, as usual, but on weekends he took his friends out east on a boat he'd bought in high school to fish and water-ski. On occasion Mary asked Freddy to take Donald with him. "Sorry, guys," he'd say to his friends, "but I have to bring my pain-in-the-ass little brother along." Donald was probably as enthusiastic as Freddy was reluctant. Whatever their father thought about his older brother, Freddy's friends clearly loved him and always had a good time—a reality that contradicted what Donald had been brought up to believe.

In August 1958, before the beginning of his junior year, Freddy and Billy Drake flew down to Nassau in the Bahamas for a short vacation before school started up again. The two of them chartered a boat and spent their days fishing and exploring the island. One evening back at their hotel, while they sat at the pool bar, Freddy met a pretty, petite blonde named Linda Clapp. Two years later, he would marry her.

That September, Donald arrived at NYMA. He went from a world in which he could do as he pleased to one in which he faced punishment for not making his bed and got slammed against the wall by upperclassmen for no particular reason. Perhaps because of having lost his own father at twelve, Fred recognized his son's isolation and visited almost every weekend between the time Donald started as an eighth grader and the time he graduated in 1964. That somewhat mitigated Donald's sense of abandonment and grievance and gave him his first glimmer that he had a connection with his father that his older brother did not. Donald's mother went occasionally but for the most part was relieved to have him gone.

Though he hadn't wanted to attend NYMA, certain things made sense for Donald there, just as ROTC had for Freddy. There was structure, and there were consequences to his actions. There was a logical system of punishment and reward. At the same time, though, life at NYMA reinforced one of Fred's lessons: the person with the power (no matter how arbitrarily that power was conferred or attained) got to decide what was right and wrong. Anything that helped you maintain power was by definition right, even if it wasn't always fair.

NYMA also reinforced Donald's aversion to vulnerability, which is essential for tapping into love and creativity because it can also expose us to shame, something he could not tolerate. By necessity he had to improve his impulse control, not only to avoid punishment but to help him get away with transgressions that required a little more finesse.

Freddy's senior year was one of the best and most productive years of his whole life. The BA in business was the least of it. He'd been made president of Sigma Alpha Mu, and he completed ROTC and would enter the Air Force National Guard as a second lieutenant after graduation. Most important, he became a fully licensed commercial pilot, although he had no intention of using the license; he was going to work with his dad in Brooklyn with every intention of someday taking over.

By the time Freddy joined Trump Management in the summer of 1960, Fred's company comprised more than forty buildings and complexes, with thousands of units, spread across Brooklyn and Queens. Fred had been taking his oldest son to construction sites for years;

his largest developments, including Shore Haven and Beach Haven in Brooklyn, as well as smaller projects closer to home in Jamaica Estates, had all been built while Freddy was growing up in the 1940s and 1950s. During those visits, the importance of cost cutting (if it's cheaper, do it yourself; if not, outsource it) and cost saving (red bricks were a penny cheaper than white bricks) were drilled into him. Fred also dragged him to meetings of the Brooklyn Democratic Party and political fund-raisers, making sure he got to know the most important and influential politicos in the city.

Now a full-time employee, Freddy started accompanying his father on rounds to the buildings, checking in with the superintendents, and overseeing repairs. Being in the field was better than being in the former dentist office where my grandfather's business was located on Avenue Z in South Brooklyn, with its cramped quarters and dim lighting. Though Fred's business was raking in millions of dollars a year, he still dealt directly with tenants when he believed the circumstances warranted doing so. If, for example, a tenant complained a little too loudly or frequently, Fred paid him or her a visit, knowing his reputation preceded him. On occasion he took Freddy along to demonstrate how to handle such situations.

When one tenant repeatedly called the office to report a lack of heat, Fred paid him a visit. After knocking on the door, he removed his suit jacket, something he usually did only right before getting into bed. Once inside the apartment, which was indeed cold, he rolled up his shirtsleeves (again, something he rarely did) and told his tenant that he didn't know what they were complaining about. "It's like the tropics in here," he told them.

Freddy began checking in for his National Guard duty. One weekend a month he had to report to the Armory in Manhattan. Fred didn't comment on those weekend absences, but he was annoyed by the two weeks a year Freddy had to take off in order to report to Fort Drum in upstate New York. For Fred, who had no use for military service, it was a waste of his employee's time.

One evening after a long day in Brooklyn, Freddy got a phone call from Linda. They hadn't spoken for more than a year. She told him that she'd become a stewardess for National Airlines and was flying out of Idlewild Airport (now John F. Kennedy International Airport). She remembered that Freddy had mentioned that his dad owned a couple of apartment buildings in Queens, and she wondered if he could help her find a place not too far from the airport. Fred had several buildings in Jamaica only a fifteen-minute bus ride from Idlewild. They found a studio at the Saxony on Highland Avenue right next to a nine-acre wooded park with a large pond in the middle of it. She moved in right away. Soon she and Freddy were dating.

A year later, in August 1961, Freddy took Linda for dinner at their favorite restaurant in Manhattan. During cocktails, he sneaked an engagement ring into Linda's glass and proposed. After dinner, they drove to Jamaica Estates to tell his parents. Fred and Mary took the news . . . calmly.

Based on Linda's modest upbringing (her father was a truck driver, and later her parents ran a clam shack near the beach in Florida) and her perceived lack of sophistication and education, they assumed that she must be a gold digger. But it was a fundamental and deliberate misunderstanding that failed to acknowledge reality; Linda probably had no idea just how wealthy her future father-in-law was. And if Linda was a gold digger, she was an exceptionally bad one.

Given her own very modest upbringing in Scotland, my grandmother could have been my mother's ally, but when Mary MacLeod had reached the top of the ladder, she had pulled it up after her. As for Fred, he simply did not like her. In any case, she was Freddy's choice, so she was suspect.

Meanwhile, the rules for stewardesses at the time were very strict:

you could be suspended for letting your hair get too long or putting on weight, and you could not continue to work if you married. After her last flight in January 1962, a couple of weeks before the wedding, Linda would have no independent income.

Because Linda's mother was confined to a wheelchair due to her advanced rheumatoid arthritis, they decided to have the wedding in Florida. A simple cocktail reception would take place at Pier Sixty-Six Hotel & Marina on the Inland Waterway in Fort Lauderdale after the church ceremony. Fred and Mary weren't pleased, but since they didn't offer to help financially, they had little say. Neither Elizabeth, who was at college in Virginia, nor Donald, who was still at NYMA, attended. The Trumps settled for hosting a reception in New York after the couple returned from their honeymoon.

Trump Village in Coney Island—the largest Trump Management project to date—was slated to break ground in 1963, and Freddy would be assisting in the preparations. Fred expected him to take an apartment in one of his Brooklyn buildings so he could be close at hand to manage any problems that cropped up, but Freddy and Linda moved instead into a one-bedroom in the city on East 56th Street between First Avenue and Sutton Place. They bought a poodle, the first pet Freddy had ever had, and a few months later Linda was pregnant.

That November, Frederick Crist Trump, III, was born. A month later, Freddy bought his first plane—a Piper Comanche 180. He and Linda flew it down to Fort Lauderdale right after Christmas to show it—and their new son—off to Linda's parents. Her father, Mike, who often parked near the runway of the Fort Lauderdale Airport to watch planes take off and land, couldn't have been more impressed.

During one of the weekly dinners Freddy and Linda had with Maryanne and her husband, David Desmond, whom she had married in 1960, Freddy told them about the plane, adding "Don't tell Dad. He wouldn't get it."

———

In September 1963, they moved into the Highlander, one of Fred's Jamaica buildings, down the block from where Linda had lived when she had first moved to town three years earlier—a stepping-stone to a house on Long Island. The Highlander was typical of Fred's buildings, having a grand entrance to distract from the substandard rental units. The lobby had a large sunken space with a formal sitting area blocked off by velvet ropes and stanchions on one side and on the other a huge display of oversized tropical plants. Between them, large floor-to-ceiling plate-glass windows looked out onto a wide expanse of flagstones and brick steps on either side curving up to the sidewalk. On either side of the steps was more extravagant foliage, towering oak trees and exotic plants with enormous dark green leaves—another Fred Trump touch. The building stood at the top of a hill on Highland Avenue, essentially the dividing line that ran through Jamaica: the north side had a more suburban feel and was predominantly white; the south side was urban and predominantly black. The front and back doors of the building gave onto two different worlds. Freddy and Linda took a two-bedroom apartment on the southeast corner of the ninth and top floor overlooking the park and Jamaica High School in the distance on one side and south Jamaica on the other.

Freddy worried at first that being the landlord's on-site son, as well as an employee of the company that owned the building, would give people an open invitation to bother him at all hours. But the building was less than fifteen years old, and the superintendent made sure the other tenants left him alone.

Not long after the move, Freddy told Linda he wanted to become a professional pilot. After three years at Trump Management he found the work a grind. Almost from the beginning, his father had frozen him out of the day-to-day operations of the Trump Village development; instead he'd been relegated to handling tenants' complaints and overseeing maintenance projects.

Being a pilot would give him a chance to do something he loved while making a good living. Before the dawn of the jet age in the early

1960s, there had been a seven-year hiring freeze on commercial pilots. With the introduction of the Boeing 707 and Douglas DC-8 into airline fleets, however, air travel exploded. Pan Am launched overseas flights in 1958 and loaned its jets to National for domestic routes. The following year, TWA, American, Delta, and United were all using jets, which, larger, more powerful, and safer to fly than their turboprop predecessors, could carry more passengers greater distances.

With the expansion in air service came a demand for qualified pilots who already had the skills necessary to train quickly on the new jets. TWA was the last airline to embrace the 707, and it was under a lot of pressure to catch up. At Idlewild and at MacArthur Airport, where Freddy kept his Comanche, the walls were plastered with notices about the need for fresh blood in commercial cockpits.

Linda said no. Having been a stewardess, she knew what pilots got up to during their layovers. For the time being, Freddy agreed to shelve the idea and make the best of life at Trump Management.

But the situation with his father deteriorated. When Freddy approached him with ideas for innovations, Fred shot him down. When he asked for more responsibility, Fred brushed him off.

Trying to prove he could make executive decisions, Freddy placed a window order for one of the older buildings. When Fred found out, he was furious. "You should have slapped a goddamn coat of paint on them instead of wasting my money!" he shouted while the employees looked on. "Donald is worth ten of you. He never would have done anything so stupid." Donald was still in high school at the time.

It was one thing for his father to humiliate him in front of his siblings, but the people in that office weren't Freddy's peers. Someday, presumably, he would be their boss. For his nascent authority to be undermined so publicly felt like a body blow.

When he got home that night, he told Linda how trapped he felt and confessed that he'd never been happy working for his father. It wasn't at all what he had expected, and for the first time it occurred to him that Trump Management might be a dead end for him. "I'm applying to TWA, Linda. I have to." He wasn't asking anymore. Fred might cut him off, but Freddy was willing to risk losing his inheritance. Pilots, especially pilots working for TWA, had good benefits and job security. He would be able to support his young family on his own, and he would be his own man.

When Freddy told his father that he was leaving Trump Management to become a commercial pilot, Fred was stunned. It was a betrayal, and he had no intention of letting his oldest son forget it.

CHAPTER FOUR

Expecting to Fly

Only the best pilots were assigned to fly the coveted Boston–Los Angeles route. And in May 1964, Freddy was on his first official flight as a professional pilot from Boston's Logan Airport to LAX—less than six months after he'd applied for a spot in that year's first training class.

What Freddy achieved in the cockpit made him unique in the Trump family. None of Fred's other children would accomplish so much entirely on their own. Maryanne came closest, putting herself through law school in the early 1970s and, over the course of nine years, compiling a solid record as a prosecutor. Her eventual appointment to the federal appeals court, however, was possible because Donald used his connections to do her a favor. For decades Elizabeth worked in the same job at Chase Manhattan Bank that Fred had arranged for her. Donald was enabled from the beginning, every one of his projects funded and supported by Fred and then by myriad other enablers right up to the present. Other than a brief stint at a New York securities firm after graduating from college, Robert worked for Donald and then his father. Even Fred was not entirely self-made, since his mother had started the business that would become Trump Management.

Freddy had put himself through flight school in college, defied his father (which he would spend the rest of his life paying for), and had no support from, as well as the active contempt of, his family. Obstacles aside, he had been determined to apply to TWA as many times as necessary. He made it on the first try.

In the 1950s and '60s, the vast majority of incoming pilots had received their training in the military; a typical training class had twenty students: four from the air force, four from the navy, four from the army, four from the marines, and four civilians. At twenty-five years old, Freddy was one of twelve men accepted into the airline's first 1964 pilots' class. Ten of them had received their training in the military. When you consider that there were no flight simulators and all the training was done in the air, the achievement was all the more staggering. Freddy was finally reaping the rewards of all of those hours he'd logged at the airfield while his fraternity brothers were partying.

In those days, air travel was at the height of its glamour, and at the forefront of that trend was Howard Hughes's Trans World Airlines, the favorite of the Hollywood glitterati. TWA provided limousines to the gossip columnists Hedda Hopper and Louella Parsons to ferry them to and from the airport; the resulting publicity made everyone want to fly TWA. One of the largest carriers in the world, TWA flew both domestically and internationally. The captain was God and treated accordingly, and thanks to Hughes's penchant for beautiful women, the stewardesses all looked like movie stars.

The reactions pilots got from passengers as they walked through the terminal, the admiring stares, the requests for autographs, were all new to Freddy and a welcome change from Trump Management, where he had struggled and failed to gain respect. The gleaming airports stood in stark contrast to the dark, unwelcoming office and dirty construction sites he'd left behind in New York. In place of bulldozers and backhoes, rows of 707s and DC-8s glimmered on the tarmac. Instead of having all of his decisions second-guessed and criticized by his father, on the flight deck Freddy had the controls.

Freddy moved his young family to Marblehead, a small harbor town forty minutes northeast of Boston's Logan Airport on the Massachusetts coast. They rented a ramshackle cottage set among an eclectic mix of houses that circled the village green not far from the sprawling harbor, where Freddy kept his "yacht," a beat-up Boston Whaler.

May in Marblehead was idyllic. Freddy loved the flying. There was a lot of socializing, with barbecues and deep-sea fishing excursions. Almost every weekend, friends came up from New York to visit them. After a month, though, Freddy started to struggle with the schedule. He was often at loose ends when he wasn't in the cockpit. Linda noticed that he started drinking more than everyone else—something that had never been a problem before.

Her husband didn't confide in Linda anymore, wanting perhaps to shield her, so she wasn't privy to the details of the conversation he'd had with Fred back in December. Linda didn't know about the constant barrage of abuse Freddy was receiving from his father in New York through letters and phone calls. But his friends knew. Freddy told them, with a note of disbelief in his voice, that the old man was embarrassed to have a "bus driver in the sky" for a son. It didn't take much for his father to convince him that choosing to leave Trump Management meant choosing failure. The most crucial thing that Linda didn't fully grasp—and to be fair, Freddy probably didn't grasp it, either—was how much Fred Trump's opinion mattered to his son.

One night, after returning from his most recent rotation, Freddy seemed particularly on edge. Over dinner, he said, "We need to get a divorce."

Linda was shocked. Her husband was under more stress than usual, but she thought it might be the result of his being responsible for the lives of more than two hundred people every time he flew.

"Freddy, what are you talking about?"

"It's not working out, Linda. I don't see how we can keep going."

"You're not even here half the time," she said, mystified by his outburst. "We have a baby. How can you say that?"

Freddy stood up and poured himself a drink. "Forget it," he said, and left the room.

They never renewed that conversation, and after a few days, they continued on as though nothing unusual had happened.

In June Donald, then eighteen and freshly graduated from the military academy, and Robert, sixteen, still a student at Freddy's alma mater, St. Paul's, drove up to Marblehead for a visit, arriving in Donald's new sports car, a high school graduation present from his parents—a step up from the luggage Freddy had received when he had graduated from college.

Freddy was anxious about seeing them. None of his siblings had ever been up in a plane with him or expressed any interest in his new career. He hoped that maybe, if he could let his brothers into his world, he'd find an ally; having even one person in his family who believed in him might bolster his waning strength to withstand his father's disapproval.

At the time of the visit, Donald was at a crossroads. When Freddy had announced he was stepping away from Trump Management in December 1963, Donald had been caught flat-footed. His brother's decision had come at the end of the first semester of Donald's senior year, and since his name wasn't Fred, he had no idea what his future role in the company might be, although he did plan to work there in some capacity. Because of that uncertainty, he hadn't adequately prepared for his future beyond high school. When he graduated from New York Military Academy that spring, he had not yet been accepted into college. He asked Maryanne to help him find a spot at a local school when he got back home.

Freddy and Linda had a barbecue for lunch, during which Donald told them he was going to Chicago with their dad to "help" him with a development he was considering. Freddy's relief was palpable. Maybe Fred was beginning to accept the new reality and had decided to take Donald on as his heir apparent.

Later in the afternoon, Freddy took the boys out on his "yacht" to do some fishing.

Despite Freddy's best attempts to teach his brother the basics of the sport, Donald had never gotten the hang of it. Donald had still been at NYMA the last time they'd been on a boat together, along with Billy and a couple of Freddy's fraternity brothers. When one of them had tried to show Donald how to hold the pole properly, Donald had pulled away and said, "I know what I'm doing."

"Yeah, buddy. And you're doing it really badly." The rest of the guys had laughed. Donald had thrown his pole onto the deck and stalked off toward the bow. He had been so angry, he wasn't paying attention to where he was walking, and Freddy had worried that he might walk right off the boat. Donald's fishing skills hadn't improved in the interim.

When the three brothers returned from the harbor, Linda was preparing dinner. As soon as they came into the house, she could sense the tension. Something had shifted. Freddy's good mood had been replaced by a quiet, barely contained anger. Freddy didn't often lose his temper, not then, and she took it as a bad sign. He poured himself a drink. Another bad sign.

Even before they sat down for dinner, Donald started in on his older brother. "You know, Dad's really sick of you wasting your life," he declared, as though he'd suddenly remembered why he was there.

"I don't need you to tell me what Dad thinks," said Freddy, who already knew his father's opinions all too well.

"He says he's embarrassed by you."

"I don't get why you care," Freddy replied. "You want to work with Dad, go ahead. I'm not interested."

"Freddy," he said, "Dad's right about you: you're nothing but a glorified bus driver." Donald may not have understood the origin of their father's contempt for Freddy and his decision to become a professional pilot, but he had the bully's unerring instinct for finding the most effective way to undermine an adversary.

Freddy understood that his brothers had been sent to deliver their father's message in person—or at least Donald had. But hearing Fred's belittling words come out of his little brother's mouth broke his spirit.

Linda overheard the exchange and came into the living room from the kitchen in time to see Freddy's face drained of all color. She slammed the plate she was holding onto the table and screamed at her brother-in-law, "You should just keep your mouth shut, Donald! Do you know how hard he's had to work? You have no idea what you're talking about!"

Freddy didn't speak to either of his brothers for the remainder of that night, and they left for New York the next morning, a day earlier than planned.

Freddy's drinking worsened.

In July, TWA offered him a promotion. The airline wanted to send him to their facility in Kansas City to train him on the new 727s it was introducing to the fleet. He declined, even though Linda reminded him that he never would have disregarded an order from one of his superiors in the National Guard. He told management that having signed a yearlong lease for a furnished house in Marblehead only two months earlier, he couldn't justify uprooting his young family again. In truth, Freddy had begun to suspect that his dream was coming to an end. He was losing hope that his father would accept him as a professional pilot, and without that acceptance he probably couldn't continue. He had spent his entire life up until he had left Trump Management trying his best to become the person his father wanted him to be. When those attempts had repeatedly ended in failure, he had hoped that in the course of fulfilling his own dream that his father would come to accept him for who he really was. He had spent his childhood navigating the minefield of his father's conditional acceptance, and he knew all too well that there was only one way to receive it—by being someone he wasn't—and he would never be able to pull that off. His father's approval still mattered more than anything else. Fred was, and always had been, the ultimate arbiter of his children's worth (which is why, even late into her seventies, my aunt Maryanne continued to yearn for her long-dead father's praise).

When TWA later offered Freddy the opportunity to fly out of Idlewild, he jumped at the chance, thinking it might be a way to salvage the situation. The move made no sense from a practical perspective, since he'd have to commute from Marblehead to New York every three or four days. Worse, it put him into closer proximity to Fred. But maybe for Freddy that was the point. Even if he couldn't get Fred's approval, it might be easier to convince his father that flying was what he should be doing if he could see it up close. In between flights, Freddy took fellow pilots back to the House to meet his family, hoping Fred might be impressed. It was a desperate move, but Freddy *was* desperate.

In the end, it made no difference. Fred could never get past the betrayal. Although Freddy had joined ROTC and a fraternity and the flying club, things his father would have disdained but probably didn't know about, those activities hadn't altered his plan to work for his father to ensure that the empire would survive in perpetuity. From Fred's perspective, Freddy's leaving Trump Management must have felt like an act of blatant disrespect. Ironically, it was the kind of boldness Fred had wanted to instill in his son, but it had been squandered on the wrong ambition. Instead, Fred felt that Freddy's unprecedented move undermined his authority and diminished Fred's sense that he was in control of everything, including the course of his son's life.

A few weeks after the boys' visit, a summer storm thundered over Marblehead Harbor. Linda was standing in the living room ironing Freddy's white uniform shirts when the phone rang. As soon as she heard her husband's voice, she knew something was wrong. He had quit his job at TWA, he told her. The three of them needed to move back to New York as soon as possible. Linda was stunned. That Freddy would give up everything he'd worked for after only four months made no sense at all.

In fact, TWA had given him an ultimatum: if he resigned, he could keep his license; otherwise, it would be forced to fire him as a result of his serious alcohol problem. If Freddy got fired, he'd likely never be able to fly again. He chose the first option, and with that their life in Marblehead was over. Just after Labor Day, the three of them moved back to the corner apartment on the ninth floor of the Highlander in Jamaica.

But Freddy hadn't entirely given up on a flying career. Maybe, he thought, if he started with smaller airlines with smaller planes and shorter, less stressful routes, he could work his way back up. While Linda and Fritz settled in, Freddy went to Utica, a small city in upstate New York, to work for Piedmont Airlines, which flew commuter routes in the northeast. That job lasted less than a month.

He moved to Oklahoma and flew for another local airline. He was there when Fritz celebrated his second birthday. By December, he was back in Queens. His drinking was out of control, and he knew that he could no longer hack it as a pilot. The only self-made man in the family, Freddy was being slowly, inexorably dismantled.

Less than a year after it had begun, Freddy's flying career was over. With no other options, he found himself standing in front of his father, who sat in his usual spot on the love seat in the library while his oldest son asked for a job that he didn't want and Fred didn't think he could do.

Fred reluctantly agreed, making it clear that he was doing his son a favor.

And then one more glimmer of hope emerged. In February 1965, Fred acquired the site of Steeplechase Park, one of three iconic amusement parks in Coney Island that had been in operation since around the turn of the twentieth century. Steeplechase had outlived its two rivals by decades: Dreamland had been destroyed by fire in 1911, and Luna Park, also struck by fires, had closed in 1944. Fred owned a building complex and shopping area named after Luna Park not far from the original site. Steeplechase continued operations until 1964. The Tilyou family had owned the park from the beginning, but several factors—including high crime and increasing competition for entertainment dollars—had persuaded them to sell the property. Fred, who had known that Steeplechase might become available for development, set his sights on its acquisition. The plan would be another residential development in the style of Trump Village, but a significant hurdle would need to be overcome: changing current zoning laws from public use to private construction. While he waited for the opportunity to present itself, Fred began to lobby his old cronies for their support and started drafting his proposal.

He dangled the possibility of Freddy's involvement in the ambitious project, and his oldest son, frantic to improve his position and put TWA behind him, jumped at the opportunity. He suspected it might be his last chance to prove himself to the old man.

By then Linda was six months pregnant with me.

PART TWO

The Wrong Side of the Tracks

CHAPTER FIVE

Grounded

Since September 1964, Donald had been living at the House and commuting thirty minutes to Fordham University in the Bronx, his attendance at which he'd avoid mentioning in the years to come. Going from the regimented life at New York Military Academy to the relatively relaxed structure of college was a tough transition for Donald, who often found himself at loose ends and spent time strutting around the neighborhood looking for girls to flirt with. One afternoon he came across Annamaria, Billy Drake's girlfriend, standing in the driveway watching her father wash the family car. Donald knew who she was, but they'd never spoken before. Annamaria knew all about Donald from Freddy. As the two of them were chatting, she mentioned that she had gone to a boarding school near New York Military Academy.

"Which one?" he asked.

When she told him, he looked at her for a second and then said, "I'm so disappointed that you went to that school."

Annamaria, who was three years older than Donald, said, "Who are you to be disappointed in me?" That ended the conversation. His idea of flirting was to insult her and act superior. It struck her as juvenile, as if he were a second grader who expressed his affection for a girl by pulling her hair.

With Freddy's apparent fall from grace, Donald saw an opportunity to take his place as their father's right-hand man at Trump Management.

Having learned his lesson to be the best—even if in ways his father hadn't intended—Donald was determined to secure a degree commensurate with his new ambitions even if it only secured him bragging rights. Fred knew nothing about the relative merits of one college over another—neither he nor my grandmother had gone to college—so the Trump kids were essentially on their own when it came to applying to schools. Aware of the Wharton School's reputation, Donald set his sights on the University of Pennsylvania. Unfortunately, even though Maryanne had been doing his homework for him, she couldn't take his tests, and Donald worried that his grade point average, which put him far from the top of his class, would scuttle his efforts to get accepted. To hedge his bets he enlisted Joe Shapiro, a smart kid with a reputation for being a good test taker, to take his SATs for him. That was much easier to pull off in the days before photo IDs and computerized records. Donald, who never lacked for funds, paid his buddy well. Not leaving anything to chance, he also asked Freddy to speak with James Nolan, a friend from St. Paul's, who happened to work in Penn's admissions office. Maybe Nolan would be willing to put in a good word for Freddy's little brother.

Freddy was happy to help, but he had an ulterior motive: though he never saw Donald as competition or thought he was out to replace him, he also didn't like to be around his increasingly insufferable younger sibling. It would be a relief to have Donald out of the way.

In the end, all of Donald's machinations may not have even been necessary. In those days, Penn was much less selective than it is now, accepting half or more of those who applied. In any case, Donald got what he wanted. In the fall of 1966, his junior year, he would transfer from Fordham to the University of Pennsylvania.

My grandfather completed the purchase of Steeplechase Park for $2.5 million in July 1965, a couple of months after I was born; a year later, Trump Management was still struggling to get the approvals and zoning it needed to move ahead. They were also battling public opposition to the project.

Freddy told his friends that nothing had changed since his previous stint at Trump Management. Fred's constant micromanaging and lack of respect for his son made what could have been an exciting challenge a grim, joyless exercise. Failure, it went without saying, would have been a disaster. Freddy still believed, though, that if he had a hand in pulling the development off, he'd be on a much better footing with his father.

That summer my parents rented a cottage in Montauk from Memorial Day through Labor Day so Dad could escape the pressure cooker in Brooklyn. Mom planned to stay with me and Fritz full-time, and Dad would fly back and forth on the weekends. The recently renamed JFK was a fifteen-minute drive from the Trump Management office, and Montauk Airport, really just a small airstrip in an open field, was right across the street from the cottage, making it an easy commute. Freddy's favorite thing to do was still fly his friends to Montauk and take them out on the water.

By the time the summer was over, my grandfather's plans for Steeplechase were in peril, and he knew it. Fred had been counting on his longtime connections to the Brooklyn Democratic machine, which had eased the way for so many of his developments in the past. By the mid-1960s, however, his political cronies were falling out of power, and it soon became clear that he wasn't going to get the rezoning he needed. Nevertheless, he made Freddy responsible for the near impossible: making Steeplechase a success.

Time was running out. Suddenly, my father, at twenty-eight, had a more public role, giving press conferences and arranging photo ops. In one picture, my dad, thin in his trench coat, stands in the foreground of a warehouse, empty and cavernous, staring into the vast space, looking small and utterly lost.

In a last-ditch effort to circumvent a push by local residents to have Steeplechase declared a landmark, which would have halted the development and scuttled his plans, Fred decided to host an event at the Pavilion of Fun, built in 1907. The purpose was to celebrate the park's demolition—in other words, he would destroy what the community was trying to save before landmark status could be secured. He had my father give a press conference in order to announce the plan, making him the face of the controversy. The extravaganza featured models in bathing suits. Guests were invited to throw bricks (available for purchase) through the iconic window featuring an enormous image of the park's mascot, Tilly, and his wide, toothy smile. In a photograph my grandfather holds a sledgehammer while grinning at a bikini-clad woman.

The entire spectacle was a disaster. Sentiment, nostalgia, and community were concepts my grandfather didn't understand, but when those windows were broken, even he must have conceded to himself that he'd gone too far. Due to local rebellion against his project, he was unable to secure the zoning change he needed and was forced to back out of the Steeplechase development.

The venture exposed his waning ability to move the ball down the field. Fred's power was largely derived from his connections. In the early to mid-1960s, there was a significant changing of the guard in New York City politics, and, as many of his old connections and cronies were losing their own power and places, Fred was being passed by. He would never again pursue an original construction project. Trump Village, completed in 1964, would be the last complex ever built by Trump Management.

Unable to accept responsibility, much as Donald would later be, Fred blamed Freddy for the failure of Steeplechase. Eventually, Freddy blamed himself.

It didn't help that Donald drove back to the House from Philadelphia almost every weekend. It turned out that he wasn't any more comfortable at Penn than he had been at Fordham. The work didn't interest him, and it's possible that he suddenly found himself a small fish in a big pond. In the 1960s, NYMA had been at the height of its enrollment—a little over five hundred students in grades eight through twelve—but Penn had several thousand when he attended. At the military academy, Donald had survived the first couple of years as an underclassman by using the considerable skills he'd acquired growing up in the family house: his ability to feign indifference in the face of pain and disappointment, to withstand the abuse of the bigger, older boys. He hadn't been a great student, but he'd had a certain charm, a way of getting others to go along with him that, back then, wasn't entirely grounded in cruelty. In high school Donald had been a decent athlete, a guy some people found attractive with his blue eyes and blond hair and his swagger. He had all the confidence of a bully who knows he's always going to get what he wants and never has to fight for it. By the time he was a senior, he had enough cachet with his fellow students that they chose him to lead the NYMA contingent in the New York City Columbus Day Parade. He didn't foresee any such success at Penn and saw no reason to spend any more time there than he had to. The prestige of the degree was what really mattered anyway.

During the most crucial juncture of the Steeplechase deal, its unraveling, and its aftermath, Donald did a fair amount of armchair quarterbacking. Freddy, who had never developed the armor that might have helped him withstand his father's mockery and humiliation, was particularly sensitive to being dressed down in front of his siblings. When they were younger, Donald had been both a bystander and collateral damage. Now that he was older, he felt increasingly confident that Freddy's continuing loss of their father's esteem would be to his benefit, so he often watched silently or joined in.

My father and grandfather were conducting a Steeplechase postmortem in the breakfast room that, on Fred's side, was acrimonious and accusatory and, on Freddy's, was defensive and remorseful. Donald casually said to his brother, as though completely unaware of the effect his words would have, "Maybe you could have kept your head in the game if you didn't fly out to Montauk every weekend."

Freddy's siblings knew that their father had always disapproved of what was now merely Freddy's hobby. There was a tacit agreement that they wouldn't talk about the planes or the boats in front of the Old Man. Fred's reaction to Donald's revelation proved the point when he said to Freddy, "Get rid of it." The next week, the plane was gone.

Fred made Freddy miserable, but Freddy's need for his father's approval seemed to intensify after Marblehead and even more after the demise of Steeplechase. He'd do whatever his father told him to do in the hope of gaining his acceptance. Whether he realized it consciously or not, it would never be granted.

When they first moved into the Highlander, Freddy and Linda had been concerned that the other tenants would bother the landlord's son with their complaints. Now they found themselves at the bottom of the list when they needed repairs.

The windows in my parents' ninth-floor corner bedroom offered expansive southern and eastern views, but they were also vulnerable to strong gusts of wind. In addition, the Highlander had built-in air conditioners in every room that hadn't been installed properly, so condensation accumulated between the drywall and outer bricks whenever the AC was running. Over time, the built-up moisture seeped into the drywall, softening it. By December, the wall around the unit in my parents' bedroom had deteriorated so badly that a frigid draft constantly blew into the room. My mother tried to cover the wall around the air conditioner with plastic sheeting, but the arctic air continued to pour in. Even with the heat blasting, their bedroom was always bitterly cold. The superintendent at the Highlander never responded to their request to have a maintenance crew sent up, and the wall was never repaired.

New Year's Eve 1967 was particularly inclement, but despite the rain and wind, my parents drove out east to celebrate with friends at Gurney's Inn in Montauk. By the time they were ready to drive back to Jamaica in the early hours of New Year's Day, the weather had turned even colder and the steady rain had become a downpour. When Freddy went outside to warm up the car, the battery was dead. Dressed only in his shirtsleeves, he got drenched trying to get the car to start. By the time he and Linda returned to the apartment and their windblown bedroom, he was sick.

Between the stress of the last two years and his heavy drinking and smoking (by then he averaged two packs of cigarettes a day), Freddy was in bad shape to begin with. His cold rapidly worsened, and after a few days he wasn't getting any better as he shivered, wrapped in a blanket, unable to escape the drafts. Linda repeatedly called the superintendent but got no response. Finally she called her father-in-law. "Please, Dad," she begged, "there must be someone who can fix this. Maybe from another building in Jamaica Estates or Brooklyn? Freddy is so sick." My grandfather suggested that she speak to the Highlander super again; there was nothing he could do.

Because for so long their life had been lived in the confines of Fred Trump's domain, it didn't occur to either one of them to hire a handyman who wasn't on Fred Trump's payroll. That wasn't how it worked in the family; Fred's permission was sought whether it was needed or not. The wall was never fixed.

A week after New Year's, Linda's father called to tell her that her mother had had a stroke. My mom didn't want to leave my father, but her mother's condition was serious, and she needed to fly down to Fort Lauderdale as soon as she could arrange child care.

Not long after, Gam called my mother to tell her that Freddy was in Jamaica Hospital with lobar pneumonia. Linda immediately got onto a plane and took a taxi straight to the hospital as soon as she landed.

My father was still in the hospital on January 20, 1967, their fifth wedding anniversary. Undeterred by his poor health and worsening alcoholism, my mother sneaked a bottle of champagne and a couple of glasses into his room. Regardless of what was happening around them or what state her husband was in, they were determined to celebrate.

Dad had been home from the hospital for only a few weeks when Linda got a call from her father. Her mother was doing better after her stroke, he told her, but he hated leaving her at the mercy of nurses while he put in full days at the quarry. The stress of work, the expense of his wife's care, and his constant worry about her were taking their toll on both of them. "I'm at the end of my rope," he said. "I don't see how we can continue."

Although Linda didn't know exactly what her father was implying, he sounded so distraught she was afraid he meant that both he and her mother would be better off dead and, out of desperation, might do something about it. When she told Freddy about her parents' precarious situation, he told her not to worry and called his father-in-law to tell him he was going to help out. "Quit your job, Mike. Take care of Mom." Money wasn't an issue, at least not then, but Freddy wasn't sure how his father would react when he told him.

"Of course," Fred said. "That's what you do for family."

My grandfather believed that in the same way he believed it was appropriate to send your kids to college or join a country club: even if it was of no interest to him or wasn't particularly important to him, it was simply "what you do."

After the Steeplechase deal collapsed, there was less for Freddy to do at Trump Management. He and Linda had been planning to buy a house since my brother had been born, and now, with extra time on his hands, they started to look for one. It didn't take long for them to find a perfect four-bedroom on a half-acre lot in Brookville, a beautiful, affluent town on Long Island. The move would add at least half an hour to Dad's commute, but a change of scenery and the freedom of being out of his father's building would do him some good. He assured the real estate agent that he could meet the asking price and getting a mortgage would be no problem.

When the bank called a few days later to tell him his mortgage application had been rejected, Freddy was stunned. With the exception of his one year with TWA, he'd been working for his father for almost six years. He was still an executive at Trump Management, which brought in tens of millions of dollars a year free and clear. In 1967, the company was worth approximately $100 million. Freddy made a decent living, he didn't have many expenses, and there was a trust fund and a (fast dwindling) stock portfolio. The most plausible explanation was that Fred, still burned by what he considered his son's betrayal and reeling from the failure of Steeplechase, had intervened in some way to prevent the transaction. My grandfather had prominent contacts and enormous accounts at Chase, Manufacturer's Hanover Trust, and the other biggest banks in the city, so not only could he guarantee that Freddy would get a mortgage, he could just as easily make sure he didn't. Our family was effectively trapped in that run-down apartment in Jamaica.

When June rolled around, my father was more than ready to spend the summer in Montauk again. My parents rented the same cottage, and with funds he raised by selling some of his blue-chip stocks, Dad bought a Chrisovich 33, which, with its sixteen-foot tuna tower, was much more suited to handle the kind of deep-sea fishing he loved. He also bought another plane, this time a Cessna 206 Stationair, which had a more powerful engine and a larger seating capacity than the Piper Comanche.

But the new toys weren't just for recreation. Dad had a plan. After Steeplechase, he had been increasingly sidelined at Trump Management, so he came up with the idea of chartering both the boat and the plane to create another source of income. If it worked out, he might be able to free himself from Trump Management after all. He hired a full-time captain to run the boat charters, but on the weekends, when doing so would have been the most lucrative, he had the captain drive him and his friends around instead.

When Linda joined them on the boat, she noticed that Freddy always drank more than everybody else, just as he had in Marblehead, which spurred increasingly intense fights between them. The increasing frequency with which Freddy flew under the influence was alarming, and as the summer of 1967 proceeded, Linda became reluctant to get onto the plane with him. The unraveling continued. By September, Dad realized that his plan wasn't going to work. He sold the boat, and when Fred found out about the plane, he got rid of that, too.

At twenty-nine years old, my father was running out of things to lose.

CHAPTER SIX

A Zero-Sum Game

I woke up to the sound of Dad's laughter. I had no sense of the time. My room was very dark, and the hallway light glared bright and incongruous under my door. I slipped out of bed. I was two and a half, and my five-year-old brother was sleeping far away on the opposite end of the apartment. I went alone to see what was going on.

My parents' room was next to mine, and its door was standing wide open. All of the lights were on. I stopped at the threshold. Dad had his back to the chest of drawers, and Mom, sitting on the bed directly across from him, was leaning away, one hand held up, the other supporting her weight on the mattress. I didn't immediately know what I was looking at. Dad was aiming a rifle at her, the .22 he kept on his boat to shoot sharks—and he kept laughing.

Mom begged him to stop. He raised the gun until it was pointing at her face. She lifted her left arm higher and screamed again, more loudly. Dad seemed to find it funny. I turned and ran back to bed.

My mother corralled my brother and me into the car and took us to a friend's house for the night. Eventually my father tracked us down. He barely remembered what he'd done, but he promised my mother it would never happen again. He was waiting for us when we returned to the apartment the next day, and they agreed to try to work things out.

But they kept going through the motions of their day-to-day lives without acknowledging the problems in their marriage. Nothing was going to get better. Things weren't even going to stay the same.

Less than two miles away, in another one of my grandfather's buildings, Maryanne was in trouble. Her husband, David, had lost his Jaguar dealership a couple of years earlier and still didn't have a job. Anybody who was paying attention would have realized that all was not well, but Maryanne's siblings and their friends thought David Desmond was a joke—rotund and harmless. Freddy had never understood the marriage or taken his brother-in-law seriously.

Maryanne had been twenty-two when she had met David. A graduate student at Columbia studying public policy, she had planned to get a PhD, but, wanting to avoid the shame of being called an old maid by her family (Freddy included), she had accepted David's proposal and dropped out of school after getting her master's degree.

The initial problem was that David, a Catholic, insisted that Maryanne convert. Not wanting to provoke her father's anger or hurt her mother's feelings, she was terrified to ask for their blessing.

When she finally did, Fred said, "Do whatever you want to do."

She explained how very, very sorry she was to disappoint them.

"Maryanne, I couldn't care less. You're going to be his wife."

Gam didn't say anything at all, and that was that.

David liked to tell Maryanne that his name would be known far beyond the reach of the Trumps. Although well educated, he didn't have any obvious skills to back up his ambition. Even so, he remained convinced that he'd find a way to succeed beyond his dreams and "show them." Like Ralph Kramden without the charm, kindness, or steady job with benefits, his "next big thing," just like the car dealership, always failed or never materialized at all. It wasn't long into the marriage before David started drinking.

The Desmonds lived rent free in a Trump apartment and enjoyed the same medical insurance everyone in the family received through

Trump Management, but free rent and medical insurance didn't put food on the table, and they had no income.

The biggest mystery, however, was why Maryanne was so financially dependent on her incompetent husband, just as it was a mystery that Elizabeth lived in a gloomy one-bedroom apartment next to the 59th Street Bridge and Freddy couldn't buy a house and his planes, boats, and luxury cars kept disappearing. My grandfather and great-grandmother had set up trust funds for all of Fred's children in the 1940s. Whether or not Maryanne was entitled to the principal yet, the trusts must have generated interest. But the three oldest children had been trained not to ask for anything ever, and if my grandfather was the trustee of those trusts, they were trapped in their financial circumstances. Asking for help meant you were weak or greedy or seeking advantage over someone who needed nothing from you in return, although an exception was made for Donald. It was so frowned upon that Maryanne, Freddy, and Elizabeth, in different ways, all suffered from totally avoidable deprivation.

After a few years of her husband's continued unemployment, Maryanne was at the end of her rope. She approached her mother, but in a way that didn't arouse suspicion. "Mom, I need some change for the laundry," she would say casually whenever she went to the House. She thought nobody knew how bad it was. For Fred, once his daughter was married, she wasn't his concern, but my grandmother knew. She didn't ask questions, either because she didn't want to pry or because she wanted Maryanne to have her "pride," and handed her daughter a Crisco can filled with dimes and quarters that came from the washers and dryers that she'd retrieved from my grandfather's buildings. Every few days, Gam made the rounds in Brooklyn and Queens, driving her pink Cadillac convertible and wearing her fox fur stole to collect the coins. As my aunt would later concede, in a family of already tremendous wealth, those Crisco cans saved her life; without them she wouldn't have been able to feed herself or her son, David, Jr.

At the very least, Maryanne should have been able to buy groceries without having to ask my grandmother, no matter how obliquely. But no matter how dire their situation, the three oldest Trump children couldn't get anybody in their family to help them in any substantive way. After a while there seemed to be no point in trying at all. Elizabeth simply accepted her lot. Dad eventually came to believe it was what he deserved. Maryanne convinced herself that not asking for or receiving help was a badge of honor. Their fear of my grandfather was so deeply ingrained that they no longer even recognized it for what it was.

The situation with David Desmond eventually became untenable. He couldn't get a job, and his drinking worsened. Desperate but being very careful not to seem as if she were asking for anything, Maryanne hinted to her father that David would love a place at Trump Management. My grandfather didn't ask if there was a problem. He gave his son-in-law a job as a parking lot attendant at one of his buildings in Jamaica Estates.

Donald graduated from the University of Pennsylvania in the spring of 1968 and went straight to work at Trump Management. From his first day on the job, my twenty-two-year-old uncle was given more respect and perks and paid more money than my father ever had been.

Almost immediately, my grandfather appointed Donald vice president of several companies that fell under the Trump Management umbrella, named him "manager" of a building he didn't actually have to manage, gave him "consulting" fees, and "hired" him as a banker.

The reasoning for that was twofold: First, it was an easy way to put Freddy in his place while signaling to the other employees that they were expected to defer to Donald. Second, it helped consolidate Donald's de facto position as heir apparent.

Donald secured his father's attention in a way nobody else did. None of Freddy's friends could understand why Donald was, in Fred's eyes, "the cat's meow." But after the summers and weekends Donald spent working for his father and visiting construction sites, Fred exposed his younger son to the ins and outs of the real estate business. Donald discovered he had a taste for the seamier side of dealing with contractors and navigating the political and financial power structures that undergirded the world of New York City real estate. Father and son could discuss the business and local politics and gossip endlessly even if the rest of us in the cheap seats had no idea what they were talking about. Not only did Fred and Donald share traits and dislikes, they had the ease of equals, something Freddy could never achieve with his father. Freddy had a wider view of the world than his brother or father did. Unlike Donald, he had belonged to organizations and groups in college that had exposed him to other people's points of view. In the National Guard and as a pilot at TWA, he had seen the best and brightest, career professionals who believed there was a greater good, that there were things more important than money, such as expertise, dedication, loyalty. They understood that life wasn't a zero-sum game. But that was part of my dad's problem. Donald was as narrow and provincial and egotistical as their father. But he also had a confidence and brazenness that Fred envied and his older brother lacked, qualities that Fred planned to turn to his advantage.

Donald's bid to replace my father at Trump Management was off to a strong start, but he was still at loose ends at home. Robert was at Boston University, which enabled him to avoid service in Vietnam, and Donald and Elizabeth didn't socialize with each other. Freddy did his best to include his little brother in whatever he and his friends got up to, but it rarely went well. They were a laid-back group who loved flying out east with Freddy to fish and water-ski. They found Donald's lack of humor and self-importance off-putting. Though they tried for Freddy's sake to welcome his little brother, they didn't like him.

Toward the end of Donald's first year at Trump Management, the tension between him and Freddy was becoming noticeable. Though Freddy tried to leave it at the office, Donald never let anything go. Despite that, when Billy Drake's girlfriend, Annamaria, was having a dinner party, Freddy asked if he could invite his brother.

The evening didn't go much better than Donald's attempted flirtation in the driveway years earlier. Shortly after the brothers arrived, raised voices drew Annamaria from the kitchen, where she was preparing dinner. She found Donald standing inches away from his brother, flushed and pointing his finger in Freddy's face. Donald looked as though he were about to hit Freddy, so Annamaria pushed herself between the two very tall men.

Freddy took a step back and said through clenched teeth, "Donald, get out of here."

Donald seemed stunned, then stormed away, saying, "Fine! You eat the girl's roast beef!" as he slammed the door on his way out.

"Idiot!" Annamaria called after him. She turned back to Freddy and asked, "What was that about?"

Shaken, Freddy simply said, "Work stuff." And they left it at that.

Things weren't getting any better at the Highlander, either. Despite my mother's fear of snakes, Dad brought home a ball python one day and put the tank into the den, forcing my mother to pass by it any time she needed to do laundry, go into my brother's room, or leave the apartment. Their fights escalated after that gratuitous bit of cruelty, and by 1970 my mother had had all she could take. She asked Dad to leave. When he came back unannounced a couple of weeks later and let himself in, she called my grandfather and insisted that the locks be changed. For once, Fred didn't object; he didn't ask any questions, and he didn't blame her. He simply told her that he would take care of it, and he did.

Dad never lived with us again.

My mother called Matthew Tosti, one of my grandfather's attorneys, to tell him she wanted a divorce. Mr. Tosti and his partner, Irwin Durben, had been doing work for my grandfather since the 1950s. Even before my parents separated, Mr. Tosti had been my mother's main contact for anything having to do with me, my brother, or money. He became her confidant; in the bleak landscape of the Trump family, he stood out as a warm and supportive ally, and she considered him a friend.

As genuinely kind as Mr. Tosti may have been, he also knew on which side his bread was buttered. Despite the fact that my mother had her own counsel, the divorce agreement might as well have been dictated by my grandfather. He knew that his daughter-in-law had no idea how much money my father's family had or what his future prospects, as the son of an exceedingly wealthy man, might be.

My mother received $100 a week in alimony plus $50 a week for child support. At the time, those weren't insignificant sums, especially considering that the big expenses, such as school, camp tuition, and medical insurance, were taken care of separately. My father was also responsible for paying the rent. Because my grandfather owned the building we lived in, it was only $90 a month. (I learned many years later that my brother and I each owned 10 percent of the Highlander, so in retrospect, charging us rent at all seems excessive.) Dad's rent obligation was capped at $250, which limited our ability to move if we ever wanted to relocate to a better apartment or neighborhood. My father, the scion of a family that *at the time* was worth well over a hundred million dollars, agreed to pay for private school and college. But Mr. Tosti had to approve our vacations. There were no marital assets to split, so my mother's total net worth was the $600 she got every month, an amount that wouldn't change over the next decade. After expenses, there was barely enough left over for Mom to contribute to her annual Christmas fund, let alone save up to buy a house.

My mother got full custody of me and my brother, as was customary at the time, but visitation rights weren't specified: "Mr. Trump shall be free to see [the children], on reasonable notice, at all reasonable times." In the vast majority of cases, visitation meant having the kids every other weekend and one night a week for dinner. That's eventually what my parents' arrangement evolved into, but at the beginning there were no formal rules.

The Steeplechase development was permanently blocked in 1969, but eventually the city purchased the land back from my grandfather. He walked away with $1.3 million in profit for having done nothing but ruin a beloved city landmark. My dad was left with nothing but the blame.

CHAPTER SEVEN

Parallel Lines

When Freddy (in 1960) and Donald (in 1968) joined Trump Management, each had a similar expectation: to become his father's right-hand man and then succeed him. They had, at different times and in different ways, been groomed to fit the part, never lacking for funds to buy expensive clothes and luxury cars. The similarities ended there.

Freddy quickly found that his father was unwilling to make room for him or delegate him any but the most mundane tasks, a problem that came to a head at the height of the construction at Trump Village. Feeling trapped, unappreciated, and miserable, he left to find his success elsewhere. At age twenty-five, he was a professional pilot, flying 707s for TWA and supporting his young family. That would turn out to be the pinnacle of Freddy's personal and professional life. At twenty-six and back at Trump Management, the chimerical chance for rehabilitation ostensibly offered to him at Steeplechase evaporated, and his prospects were at an end.

By 1971, my dad had been working for my grandfather, with the exception of his ten months as a pilot, for eleven years. Nonetheless, Fred promoted Donald, then only twenty-four, to the position of president of Trump Management. He'd been on the job for only three years and had very little experience and even fewer qualifications, but Fred didn't seem to mind.

The truth was, Fred Trump didn't need either one of his sons at

Trump Management. He promoted himself to CEO, but nothing about his job description changed: he was a landlord. Fred hadn't been a developer since the failure of Steeplechase six years earlier, so Donald's role as president remained amorphous. In the early 1970s, with New York City on the brink of economic collapse, the federal government was cutting back on the FHA (in large part because of the cost of the Vietnam War), so no more FHA funding was available to Fred. Mitchell-Lama, a New York State–sponsored program to provide affordable housing that funded Trump Village, also ground to a halt.

As a business move, promoting Donald was pointless. What exactly was he being promoted to do? My grandfather had no development projects, the political power structure he'd depended on for decades was unraveling, and New York City was in dire financial straits. The main purpose of the promotion was to punish and shame Freddy. It was the latest in a long line of such punishments, but it was almost certainly the worst, especially given the context in which it happened.

Fred was determined to find a role for Donald. He had begun to realize that although his middle son didn't have the temperament for the day-to-day attention to detail that was required to run his business, he had something more valuable: bold ideas and the chutzpah to realize them. Fred had long harbored aspirations to expand his empire across the river into Manhattan, the Holy Grail of New York City real estate developers. His early career had demonstrated that he had a knack for self-promotion, dissembling, and hyperbole. But as the first-generation son of German immigrants, Fred had English as his second language and he needed to improve his communication skills— he had taken the Dale Carnegie course for a reason, and it wasn't to boost his self-confidence. But the course had been a failure. And there was another obstacle, perhaps even more difficult to overcome: Fred's mother, as forward thinking as she had been in some ways, was generally very austere and traditional. It was okay for her son to be successful and rich. It was not okay for him to show off.

Donald had no such restraint. He hated Brooklyn as much as Freddy did but for very different reasons—the bleak working-class smallness of it, the lack of "potential." He couldn't get out of there fast enough. Trump Management was located on Avenue Z, right in the middle of Beach Haven in South Brooklyn, one of my grandfather's largest apartment complexes. He hadn't made many alterations. The narrow outer office was crammed with too many desks, and the small windows admitted little light. If Donald had thought of the surrounding buildings and complexes in terms of number of units, the value of the ground leases, and the sheer volume of income that poured into Trump Management every month, he would have recognized the huge opportunity. Instead, whenever he stood outside the office and surveyed the utilitarian sameness of Beach Haven, he must have felt suffocated by the sense that it was all beneath him. A future in Brooklyn wasn't what he wanted for himself, and he was determined to get out as quickly as possible.

Besides being driven around Manhattan by a chauffeur whose salary his father's company paid, in a Cadillac his father's company leased to "scope out properties," Donald's job description seems to have included lying about his "accomplishments" and allegedly refusing to rent apartments to black people (which would become the subject of a Justice Department lawsuit accusing my grandfather and Donald of discrimination).

Donald dedicated a significant portion of his time to crafting an image for himself among the Manhattan circles he was desperate to join. Having grown up a member of the first television generation, he had spent hours watching the medium, the episodic nature of which appealed to him. That helped shape the slick, superficial image he would come to both represent and embody. His comfort with portraying that image, along with his father's favor and the material security his father's wealth afforded him, gave him the unearned confidence to pull off what even at the beginning was a charade: selling himself not just as a rich playboy but as a brilliant, self-made businessman.

In those early days, that expensive endeavor was being enthusiastically, if clandestinely, funded by my grandfather. Fred didn't immediately realize the scope of Donald's limitations and had no idea that he was essentially promoting a fiction, but Donald was happy to spend his father's money either way. For his part, Fred was determined to keep money pouring into his son's pocket. In the late 1960s, for example, Fred developed a high-rise for the elderly in New Jersey, a project that was in part an exercise in how to get government subsidies (Fred received a $7.8 million, practically interest-free loan to cover 90 percent of the cost of the project's construction) and in part an example of how far he was willing to go to enrich his second son. Although Donald put no money toward the development costs of the building, he received consulting fees, and he was paid to manage the property, a job for which there were already full-time employees on site. That one project alone netted Donald tens of thousands of dollars a year despite his having done essentially nothing and having risked nothing to develop, advance, or manage it.

In a similar sleight of hand, Fred bought Swifton Gardens, an FHA project originally costing $10 million to build, at auction for $5.6 million. In addition, he secured a $5.7 million mortgage, which also covered the cost of upgrades and repairs, essentially paying zero dollars for the buildings. When he later sold the property for $6.75 million, Donald got all of the credit and took most of the profits.

My dad's dream of flying had been taken away from him, and he had now lost his birthright. He was no longer a husband; he barely saw his kids. He had no idea what was left for him or what he was going to do next. He did know that the only way for him to retain any self-respect was to walk away from Trump Management, this time for good.

Dad's first apartment after he moved out of the Highlander was a studio in the basement of a brick row house on a quiet, shady street in Sunnyside, Queens. He was thirty-two years old and had never lived on his own.

The first thing we saw when we walked through the door was a tank holding two garter snakes and a terrarium with a ball python.

Another tank stocked with goldfish, and another with a few mice scrambling around in the straw, were set up on stands to the left of the snakes. I knew what the mice were for.

In addition to a fold-out couch, a small kitchen table with a couple of cheap chairs, and the TV, there were two more terrariums housing an iguana and a tortoise. We called them Tomato and Izzy.

Dad seemed proud of his new place, and he kept adding to the menagerie. On one visit, he took us down to the boiler room and led us to a cardboard box with six ducklings inside. The landlord had let him set up some heat lamps, creating a makeshift incubator. They were so tiny that we had to feed them with an eyedropper.

"Just give it a quarter of a turn on the mental carburetor," my grandfather said to my father, as if that were all it would take for his son to stop drinking. As if it were just a matter of willpower. They were in the library, but for once they sat across from each other—not equals exactly, never equals—but as two people who had a problem to solve, even though they might never agree on the solution. Although the medical view of alcoholism and addiction had changed drastically in the previous few decades, public perception hadn't evolved much. Despite treatment programs such as Alcoholics Anonymous, which had been around since 1935, the stigma attached to addicts and addiction persisted.

"Just make up your mind, Fred," my grandfather said, offering a useless platitude that Norman Vincent Peale would have approved of. The closest thing Fred had to a philosophy was the prosperity gospel, which he used like a blunt instrument and an escape hatch, and it had never harmed any of his children more than it did right then.

"That's like telling me to make up my mind to give up cancer," Dad said. He was right, but my grandfather wholeheartedly embraced the "blame the victim" mentality that was still pervasive and couldn't make that leap.

"I need to beat this, Dad. I don't think I can do it by myself. I know I can't."

Instead of asking "What can I do for you?" Fred said, "What do you want from me?"

Freddy had no idea where to start.

My grandfather had never been sick a day in his life; he had never missed a day of work; he had never been sidelined by depression or anxiety or heartbreak, not even when his wife was near death. He appeared to have no vulnerabilities at all and therefore couldn't recognize or sanction them in other people.

He had never handled Gam's injuries and illnesses well. Whenever Gam was suffering, my grandfather would say something like "Everything's great. Right, Toots? You just have to think positive," and then leave the room as quickly as possible, leaving her alone to deal with her pain.

Sometimes Gam forced herself to say, "Yes, Fred." Usually she said nothing, clenched her jaw, and struggled to keep from crying. My grandfather's relentless insistence that everything was "great" left no room for any other feelings.

We were told that Dad was sick and would be in the hospital for a few weeks. We were also told that he had to give up his apartment— apparently the landlord wanted to rent the place to somebody else. Fritz and I went to pack up clothes, games, and other odds and ends we'd left behind, and when we arrived, the place was almost completely empty. The tanks were gone, the snakes were gone. I never found out what happened to them.

When Dad returned from wherever he had been—the hospital or rehab—he moved into my grandparents' attic. It was a temporary arrangement, and no effort was made to turn it into a proper living space. All of the storage boxes and old toys—including the vintage fire engine, crane, and dump truck my grandmother had hidden there all those years ago—had simply been pushed to one end of the attic and a cot set up in the cleared space at the other. Dad put his portable six-

inch black-and-white television on his old National Guard trunk beneath the dormered window.

When Fritz and I visited him, we camped out on the floor next to
his cot, and the three of us watched an endless stream of old movies
such as *Tora! Tora! Tora!* and *It's a Mad, Mad, Mad, Mad World.* When
he was well enough to come downstairs, Dad joined us on Sundays for
the weekly Abbott and Costello movie on WPIX.

After a month or two, my grandfather told Dad there was a va-
cancy in Sunnyside Towers, a building my grandfather had bought in
1968—a one-bedroom apartment on the top floor.

As Dad was preparing to move to Sunnyside, Maryanne, with the
help of a $600 loan, was getting ready to start her studies at Hof-
stra Law School. Although not her first choice, Hofstra was only
a ten-minute drive from Jamaica Estates—close enough that she
could still take my cousin David to school in the morning and pick
him up in the afternoon. Going back to school was a long-deferred
dream. She also hoped that becoming a lawyer would give her the
financial wherewithal to leave her husband someday. Their situation had become increasingly dire over the years. The parking
lot attendant job that his father-in-law had given him was a humiliation from which he hadn't recovered. Over the years, David
had lashed out at his wife from time to time, particularly when he
was drunk.

Maryanne's move toward independence sent her husband even further over the edge, and after she returned home from her first day at
law school, her husband, in a fit of rage, threw their thirteen-year-old
son out of the apartment. Maryanne took him to the House, and they
spent the night there. David Desmond, Sr., cleaned out their meager
joint savings account and left town.

When the whole family was together, we spent most of our time in
the library, a room without books until Donald's ghostwritten *The*

Art of the Deal was published in 1987. The bookshelves were used instead to display wedding photos and portraits. The wall across from the bay window overlooking the backyard was dominated by a studio portrait of the five siblings taken when they were adults that had replaced an earlier version of the five in similar poses taken when Freddy was fourteen. The only nonstudio photographs in the room were a black-and-white shot of my grandmother, looking regal and condescending in her hat and fur stole as she and my aunts, young girls at the time, descended the air stairs to the tarmac in Stornoway on the Isle of Lewis, where Gam had been born, and one of Donald in his New York Military Academy dress uniform leading the school contingent in the New York City Columbus Day Parade. There were two love seats upholstered in dark-blue-and-green vinyl against the walls and one large chair in front of the TV, a spot the kids fought over regularly. My grandfather, dressed in his three-piece suit and tie, sat on the love seat nearest the heavy pine phone table by the door, his feet planted squarely on the ground.

Every Saturday, if we weren't in Sunnyside with Dad, Fritz and I rode our bikes down Highland Avenue and along the back streets of Jamaica Estates to the House to hang out with our cousin David—or rather, Fritz and David hung out and I followed them around, trying to keep up.

Gam sat with Maryanne and Elizabeth whenever they visited at a small sky blue Formica table with stainless steel edging that looked as though it came straight out of a 1950s malt shop. Just past it, there was a dark pantry the size of a walk-in closet with a little desk where Gam kept her shopping lists, receipts, and bills. Marie, the long-suffering housekeeper, often hid there, listening to her portable radio, and on rainy or cold days when David, Fritz, and I were confined to the House, we drove her crazy. On the other side of the pantry, a swinging door led to the dining room. We used the loop that ran from the back door hallway past the kitchen, through the foyer, around to the dining room, through the pantry, and back to the kitchen as our personal racetrack, chasing one another, wiping out, screaming, gaining speed, one of us invariably banging into a piece of furniture. Between the refrigerator and the pantry doorway, Gam generally gave us free rein, but when she was in the kitchen, she would lose her patience and yell at us to stop. She threatened us with the wooden spoon if we ignored her—the sound of the drawer opening was enough to give us pause. But if we were stupid enough to keep running around her and making a racket, the spoon came out, and whoever was closest at hand got whacked. Liz did her part to slow us down by grabbing our hair as we passed by.

After that Fritz, David, and I usually ran to the basement—adults passed through only on their way to the laundry room or the garage, so we were free to be loud and to kick around the soccer ball or take turns riding up and down on (or fighting over) Gam's electric stair lift. We spent most of our time in the open space at the far end with all the lights on. With the exception of my grandfather's life-sized wooden Indian chief statues that were lined up against the far wall like sarcophagi, it was a pretty typical basement: drop ceiling with fluorescent lighting, white-and-black linoleum tile, and an old upright piano that stood largely ignored because it was so badly out of tune it wasn't even worth playing. Donald's marching hat with the huge plume that he had worn during color guard at NYMA sat on top of it. Sometimes I put it on, though it slid down to the bridge of my nose, and fastened the strap beneath my chin.

When I was down there by myself, the basement—half illuminated, the wooden Indians standing sentinel in the shadows—became a weirdly exotic space. Across from the stairs, a huge mahogany bar, fully stocked with barstools, dusty glasses, and a working sink but no alcohol, had been built in the corner—an anomaly in a house built by a man who didn't drink. A large oil painting of a black singer with beautiful, full lips and generous, swaying hips hung on the wall behind it. Wearing a curve-hugging gold-and-yellow dress with ruffles, she stood at the microphone, mouth open, hand extended. A jazz band made up entirely of black men dressed in white dinner jackets and black bow ties played behind her. The brasses glowed, the woodwinds glistened. The clarinetist, a sparkle in his eyes, looked straight out at me. I would stand behind the bar, towel slung over my shoulder, whipping up drinks for my imaginary customers. Or I would sit on one of the barstools, the only patron, dreaming myself inside that painting.

Our uncle Rob, who wasn't that much older than we were and seemed more like a sibling than an uncle, played soccer with us in the backyard whenever he came out from the city. We played hard and on hot days made frequent trips to the kitchen for a can of Coke or a grape juice. Rob would often grab a block of Philadelphia cream cheese; leaning against the refrigerator, he'd peel back the foil and eat the cream cheese as if it were a candy bar, then wash it down with soda.

Rob was a very good soccer player, and I tried to keep up with the boys, but it sometimes felt as though he used me for target practice.

When Donald was at the House, we mostly threw a baseball or football around. He had played baseball at New York Military Academy and was even less likely to pull his punches than Rob; he saw no reason to throw the ball any more gently just because his niece and nephews were six or nine or eleven. When I did manage to catch the ball he threw at me, the report of it against my leather glove reverberated off the brick retaining wall like a shot. Even with little kids, Donald had to be the winner.

Only the most dedicated optimist could have lived in Sunnyside Towers without losing hope. There was no doorman, and the plastic plants and flowers that filled the two large planters on either side of the plexiglass front door were perpetually coated in a thin film of dust. Our sixth-floor hallway reeked of stale cigarette smoke. The dank carpet was a soulless shade of seal grey. The indifferent overhead lighting hid nothing.

The height of my father's lifestyle had been when he and my mom had lived in their one-bedroom near Sutton Place right after they were married. During that year, they had spent their evenings going to the

Copacabana with friends and flying to Bimini on weekends. It had been all downhill from there, a trajectory that mirrored that of Donald, whose own lifestyle became more extravagant as the years passed. Donald had already been living in Manhattan when he married Ivana. After the wedding, they lived in a two-bedroom apartment on Fifth Avenue, then in an eight-bedroom apartment also on Fifth Avenue. Within five years they were living in the $10 million penthouse triplex in Trump Tower, all while Donald was still effectively on my grandfather's payroll.

My grandfather created Midland Associates in the 1960s to benefit his children, each of whom was given 15 percent ownership in eight buildings, one of which was Sunnyside Towers. The express purpose of this apparently quasi-legal, if not outright fraudulent, transfer of wealth was to avoid paying the lion's share of the gift taxes that would have been assessed if it had been an aboveboard transaction. I don't know if Dad knew that he owned part of the building he now lived in, but in 1973 his share of it would have been worth about $380,000, or 2.2 million in today's dollars. He seemed to have no apparent access to any of the money—his boats and planes were gone; his Mustang and Jaguar were gone. He still had his FCT vanity plates, but now they were attached to a beat-up Ford LTD. Whatever wealth my father had was by then entirely theoretical. Either his access to his trust funds had been blocked, or he had stopped thinking he had any right to his own money. Thwarted one way or the other, he was at his father's mercy.

Dad and I were watching a Mets game on television when the intercom buzzed. Dad looked surprised and went to answer. I didn't hear who was calling from the lobby, but I heard my father say "Shit" under his breath. We'd been having a laid-back afternoon, but Dad seemed tense now. "Donald's coming up for a couple of minutes," he told me.

"Why?"

"No idea." He seemed annoyed, which was unusual for him.

Dad tucked his shirt in and opened the door as soon as the bell rang. He took a couple of steps back to let his brother pass. Donald was wearing a three-piece suit and shiny shoes and carrying a thick manila envelope wrapped with several wide rubber bands. He walked into the living room. "Hi, Honeybunch," he said when he saw me.

I waved at him.

Donald turned back to my dad and said, "Jesus, Freddy," as he looked around disdainfully. My father let it slide. Donald tossed the envelope onto the coffee table and said, "Dad needs you to sign these and then bring them to Brooklyn."

"Today?"

"Yeah. Why? You busy?"

"You take it to him."

"I can't. I'm on my way to the city to look at some properties that are in foreclosure. It's a fantastic time to take advantage of losers who bought at the height of the market."

Freddy never would have dared develop his own projects outside of Brooklyn. A few years earlier on a weekend trip to the Poconos, as he and Linda had driven past row after row of condemned buildings on either side of the Cross Bronx Expressway, she'd pointed out that he could start his own business and renovate buildings in the Bronx.

"No way I could go against Dad," Freddy had said. "It's all about Brooklyn for him. He'd never go for it."

Now Donald looked out the window and said, "Dad's going to need somebody in Brooklyn. You should go back."

"And do what, exactly?" Dad scoffed.

"I don't know. Whatever you used to do."

"I had your job."

In the uncomfortable silence, Donald looked at his watch. "My driver's waiting downstairs. Get this to Dad by four o'clock, okay?"

After Donald left, Dad sat on the couch next to me and lit a cigarette. "So, kiddo," he said, "want to take a ride to Brooklyn?"

When we visited the office, Dad made the rounds on his way to Amy Luerssen, my grandfather's secretary and gatekeeper (and also my godmother), whose desk stood right outside of her boss's door. Aunt Amy clearly adored the man she called "my Freddy."

My grandfather's private office was a square room with low lighting, its walls covered with plaques and framed certificates, a lot of wooden busts of Indian chiefs in full headdress scattered about. I sat behind his desk and chose from what seemed an endless supply of blue Flair markers and the same thick pads of cheap scratch paper he had at the House, writing notes and drawing until it was time to go to lunch. When I was left alone, I spun wildly in his chair.

My grandfather always took us to eat at Gargiulo's, a formal restaurant with crisp cloth napkins and tablecloths where he went almost every day. The deferential waiters knew him, always called him "Mr. Trump," pulled out his chair, and generally fussed over him throughout the meal. It was better when Aunt Amy or somebody else from the office joined us because it took the pressure off Dad; he and my grandfather had little left to say to each other. It didn't happen often that Donald was at the office at the same time we were, but it was much worse when we crossed paths. He acted as though he owned the place, which my grandfather seemed not only to encourage but to enjoy. My grandfather was transformed in Donald's presence.

In 1973, the Department of Justice Civil Rights Division sued Donald and my grandfather for violating the 1968 Fair Housing Act by refusing to rent to *die Schwarze*, as my grandfather put it. It was one of the largest federal housing discrimination suits ever brought, and the notorious attorney Roy Cohn offered to help. Donald and Cohn had crossed paths at Le Club, a swanky members-only restaurant and disco on East 55th Street that was frequented by Vanderbilts and Kennedys, an array of international celebrities, and minor royalty. Cohn was more than a decade removed from his disastrous involvement in Joseph McCarthy's failed anti-Communist crusade. He'd been forced to resign from his position as the senator's chief counsel, but not until he'd wrecked the lives and careers of dozens of men because of their alleged homosexuality and/or ties to communism.

Like many men of his vicious temperament and with his influential connections, Cohn was subject to no rules. Embraced by a certain segment of the New York elite and hired by a diverse pool of clients such as Rupert Murdoch, John Gotti, Alan Dershowitz, and the Roman Catholic Archdiocese of New York, Cohn entered private practice back in New York City, where he'd grown up. Over the ensuing years, he became very rich, very successful, and very powerful.

Though Cohn was flashy where Fred was conservative and loud where Fred was taciturn, the differences between them were really of degree, not kind. Cohn's cruelty and hypocrisy were more public, but Fred had, in the intimate context of his family, also mastered those arts. Fred had also primed Donald to be drawn to men such as Cohn, as he would later be drawn to authoritarians such as Vladimir Putin and Kim Jong-un or anyone else, really, with a willingness to flatter and the power to enrich him.

Cohn recommended that Trump Management file a countersuit against the Justice Department for $100 million over what he alleged were the government's false and misleading statements about his clients. The maneuver was simultaneously absurd, flashy, and effective, at least in terms of the publicity it garnered; it was the first time that Donald, at twenty-seven, had landed on a newspaper's front page. And although the countersuit would be tossed out of court, Trump Management settled the case. There was no admission of wrongdoing, but they did have to change their rental practices to avoid discrimination. Even so, both Cohn and Donald considered it a win because of all the press coverage.

When Donald hitched his fortunes to the likes of Roy Cohn, the only things he had going for him were Fred's largesse and a carefully cultivated but delusional belief in his own brilliance and superiority. Ironically, the defenses he had developed as a young child to protect himself against the indifference, fear, and neglect that had defined his early years, along with his being forced to watch the abuse of Freddy, primed him to develop what his older brother clearly lacked: the ability to be the "killer" and proxy his father required.

There's no way to know precisely when Fred started to notice Donald, but I suspect it was after he shipped his son off to military school. Donald seemed amenable to his father's exhortations to be tough, a "killer," and he proved his worth by bragging about the random beatings he received from the upperclassmen or pretending not to care about his exile from home. Fred's growing confidence in Donald created a bond between them and an unshakable self-confidence in Donald. After all, the most important person in the family, the only one whose opinion mattered, was finally showing him favor. And unlike Freddy, the attention Donald received from his father was positive.

After college, when Donald was finally out in the world using his father's connections to make more connections and using his father's money to create his image as a burgeoning Master of the Universe, Fred knew that anything his son got credit for would redound to his own benefit. After all, if Donald was embraced as an up-and-coming dealmaker, that was entirely to the credit of Fred Trump—even if Fred was the only person who knew it.

In interviews in the early 1980s, Fred claimed that Donald's success had far exceeded his own. "I gave Donald free rein," he said. "He has great visions, and everything he touches seems to turn to gold. Donald is the smartest person I know." None of that was true, and Fred must have known that a decade before he said it.

After Steeplechase, Fred had lost a lot of ground. If he wanted to expand the reach of his empire, he would need a new playing field and a surrogate. He needed Donald to go out in the world and create the brand. It hadn't taken Fred long to realize that his profligate middle son wasn't suited to the unglamorous, tightly budgeted, and highly regimented routine of running rental properties. But with his father's backing, maybe he could use his hubris and shamelessness to make the push into Manhat-

tan. Fred wasn't living vicariously; he was intimately involved in all aspects of Donald's early forays into the Manhattan market, getting things
done behind the scenes while Donald played to the crowd up front. Fred
made it possible for Donald to play a role that fulfilled his own desire for
recognition while allowing his son to garner the reputation as a Manhattan developer that Fred had always aspired to. Fred would never get the
public recognition, but it was enough for him to know that the opportunities Donald had to make his mark and promote himself would never
have materialized without him. The success and the acclaim were due
to Fred and his vast wealth. Any story about Donald was really a story
about Fred. Fred also knew that if that secret was uncovered, the ruse
would fall apart. In retrospect, Fred was the puppeteer, but he couldn't
be seen to be pulling his son's strings. It's not that Fred was overlooking
Donald's incompetence as a businessman; he knew he had more than
enough talent in that arena for both of them. Fred was willing to stake
millions of dollars on his son because he believed he could leverage the
skills Donald did have—as a savant of self-promotion, shameless liar,
marketer, and builder of brands—to achieve the one thing that had always eluded him: a level of fame that matched his ego and satisfied his
ambition in a way money alone never could.

When things turned south in the late 1980s, Fred could no longer
separate himself from his son's brutal ineptitude; the father had no
choice but to stay invested. His monster had been set free. All he could
do was mitigate the damage, keep the cash flowing, and find somebody
else to blame.

Over the next two years, Dad became more taciturn, more grim, and, if
possible, thinner. The apartment in Sunnyside Towers was grey—grey
because of the northwest exposure, grey from the unending clouds of
cigarette smoke, grey because of his terrible moods. There were morn-
ings when he barely managed to get out of bed, let alone spend a whole
day with us. Sometimes he was hungover; sometimes it was his depression, which grew heavier. If we didn't have anything scheduled, Dad

often made an excuse to leave us alone, saying he had to work or run an errand for Gam.

Once Dad told us he had a job managing paperboys. I'd briefly had a paper route, and as far as I could tell that meant he was the guy who handed out the papers to the delivery kids from the trunk of his car, then collected the cash from them when they'd finished their routes. He told me once that he made $100 a day, which seemed like an enormous sum to me.

One evening, we were at the apartment having dinner with Dad's girlfriend, Johanna. I preferred it when she wasn't there; something about her was off-putting. She didn't connect—or even try to—with me and Fritz. It was bad enough that she said things such as "Freddy, light me a fag," considering she wasn't British, but Dad started saying them, too.

We'd just finished eating when I started to recount the adventures I'd had with my mother at the bank that afternoon. While she had waited in the very long line, I had stood at one of the counters and filled out deposit slips with all sorts of aliases and wild sums of money I planned to withdraw in order to fund various schemes. I could barely contain how funny I thought the whole thing was. But as I told them about the secret identities, the secret withdrawals of cash, and my fiendish plots to disperse them, Dad got a wary look in his eyes.

"Does Mr. Tosti know about this?" he asked.

If I'd been paying closer attention, I might have known to stop, but I thought he was kidding, so I kept telling my story.

Dad got increasingly agitated, leaned forward, and pointed his finger at me. "What did you do?" As moody as my father could be, I'd rarely seen him so angry, and I'd almost never heard him raise his voice. I was confused and tried to retrace my narrative back to the point where he had started to think I'd done something wrong. But there *was* no such point, and my explanation about what had really happened only agitated him further.

"If Mr. Tosti finds out about this, I'm going to be in trouble with your grandfather."

Johanna put her hand on Dad's arm, as if to draw his attention away from me. "Freddy," she said, "it's nothing."

"What do you mean 'nothing'? This is really goddamn serious."

I flinched at the curse word.

At that point both Johanna and I knew there was no talking him down. He was drunk and trapped in some old narrative. I tried to explain it to him, to steady him, but he was too far gone. And I was only eight.

In the summer of 1975, Donald gave a press conference during which he presented a rendering of the architect's plans for the Grand Hyatt, as if he'd already won the contract to replace the old Commodore Hotel next door to Grand Central Terminal on 42nd Street. The media printed his claims as fact.

That same summer, just before Fritz and I were scheduled to leave for camp, Dad had told Mom that he had some news. She invited him to dinner. I answered the door when Dad rang the bell. He was wearing what he almost always wore—black slacks and a white dress shirt— but his clothes were crisp and his hair was slicked back. I had never seen him look so handsome.

While Mom tossed the salad, Dad grilled the steak on our small terrace. When the food was ready, we sat at the small table next to the terrace, propping the door open so the mild summer breeze could blow in. We drank water and iced tea.

"I'm moving to West Palm Beach at the end of the summer," he told us. "I found a great apartment on the Intracoastal with a dock in the back." He already had a boat picked out, and when we visited, he'd take us fishing and waterskiing. As he spoke, he seemed happy and confident—and relieved. All of us knew it was the right decision; for the first time in a very long time, we felt hope.

CHAPTER EIGHT

Escape Velocity

I sat at the dining room table with the shoe in front of me, trying to figure out what the point of it was. I had looked through the remaining boxes under the tree, thinking that perhaps the shoe's twin had been wrapped separately, but no, there was just the one—a gold lamé shoe with a four-inch heel filled with hard candy. Both the individual candies and the shoe itself were wrapped in cellophane. Where had this thing come from? I wondered. Had it been a door prize or a party favor from a luncheon?

Donald came through the pantry from the kitchen. As he passed me, he asked, "What's that?"

"It's a present from you."

"Really?" He looked at it for a second. "Ivana!" he shouted into the foyer. She was standing on the other side of the Christmas tree near the living room. "Ivana!"

"What is it, Donald?"

"This is great." He pointed at the shoe, and she smiled. Maybe he thought it was real gold.

It had all started in 1977 with a three-pack of Bloomie's underwear, retail $12, my very first Christmas present from Donald and his new wife, Ivana. That same year, they had given Fritz a leather-bound journal. It looked as though it were meant for somebody older, but it was really nice, and I felt a bit slighted until we realized that it was two years out of date. At least the underwear wouldn't expire.

On holidays, Donald and Ivana pulled up to the House in either an expensive sports car or a chauffeur-driven limo that was even longer than my grandfather's. They swept into the foyer like socialites, Ivana in her furs and silk and outrageous hair and makeup, Donald in his expensive three-piece suits and shiny shoes, everyone else looking conservative and unfashionable by comparison.

I grew up thinking that Donald had struck out on his own and single-handedly built the business that had turned my family name into a brand and that my grandfather, provincial and miserly, cared only about making and keeping money. On both counts, the truth was vastly different. A *New York Times* article published on October 2, 2018, that uncovered the vast amounts of alleged fraud and quasi-legal and illegal activities my family had engaged in over the course of several decades included this paragraph:

> Fred Trump and his companies also began extending large loans and lines of credit to Donald Trump. Those loans dwarfed what the other Trumps got, the flow so constant at times that it was as if Donald Trump had his own Money Store. Consider 1979, when he borrowed $1.5 million in January, $65,000 in February, $122,000 in March, $150,000 in April, $192,000 in May, $226,000 in June, $2.4 million in July and $40,000 in August, according to records filed with New Jersey casino regulators.

In 1976, when Roy Cohn suggested that Donald and Ivana sign a prenuptial agreement, the terms set for Ivana's compensation were based on Fred's wealth because at the time Donald's father was his only source of income. I heard from my grandmother that, in addition to alimony and child support as well as the condo, the prenup, at Ivana's insistence, included a "rainy day" fund of $150,000. My parents' divorce agreement had also been based on my grandfather's wealth, but Ivana's $150,000 bonus was worth almost twenty-one years of the $600-per-month checks my mother received for child support and alimony.

Before Ivana, there had always been a sameness to the holidays that made them blur together. Christmas when I was five was indistinguishable from Christmas when I was eleven. The routine never varied. We'd enter the House through the front door at 1:00 p.m., dozens of packages in tow, handshakes and air kisses all around, then gather in the living room for shrimp cocktail. Like the front door, we used the living room only twice a year. Dad came and went, but I have no recollection of his being there one way or another.

Thanksgiving and Christmas dinners were identical, although one Christmas, Gam had the temerity to make roast beef instead of turkey. It was a meal everybody liked, but Donald and Robert were pissed off. Gam spent the whole meal with her head bowed, hands in her lap. Just when you thought the subject was dropped for good, one of them would say some version of "Jesus, Mom, I can't believe you didn't make turkey."

Once Ivana became a part of the family, she joined Donald at the power center of the table, where he sat at my grandfather's right hand, his only equal. The people nearest to them (Maryanne and Robert and Ivana) formed a claque with one mission: to prop Donald up, follow his lead in conversation, and defer to him as though nobody was as important as he was. I think that initially, it was simply an expedient—Maryanne and Robert had learned early on that there was no point in contradicting their father's obvious preference. "I never challenged my father," Maryanne said. "Ever." It was easier to go along for the ride. Donald's chiefs of staff are prime examples of this phenomenon. John Kelly, at least for a while, and Mick Mulvaney, without any reservations at all, would behave the same way—until they were ousted for not being sufficiently "loyal." That's how it always works with the sycophants. First they remain silent no matter what outrages are committed; then they make themselves complicit by not acting. Ultimately, they find they are expendable when Donald needs a scapegoat.

Over time, the discrepancy between Fred's treatment of Donald and his other children became painfully clear. It was simpler for Rob and Maryanne to toe the party line in the hope that they wouldn't get treated any worse, which seems to be the same calculation Republicans in Congress make every day now. They also knew what had happened to my father when he failed to meet Fred's expectations. The rest of us at the other end of the table were superfluous; our job was to fill the cheap seats.

A year after the gold lamé shoe, the gift basket I received from Donald and Ivana hit the trifecta: it was an obvious regift, it was useless, and it demonstrated Ivana's penchant for cellophane. After unwrapping it, I noticed, among the tin of gourmet sardines, the box of table water crackers, the jar of vermouth-packed olives, and a salami, a circular indentation in the tissue paper that filled the bottom of the basket where another jar had once been. My cousin David walked by and, pointing at the empty space, asked, "What was that?"

"I have no idea. Something that goes with these, I guess," I said, holding up the box of crackers.

"Probably caviar," he said, laughing. I shrugged, having no idea what caviar was.

I grabbed the basket handle and walked toward the pile of presents I'd stacked next to the stairs. I passed Ivana and my grandmother on the way, lifted the basket, said, "Thanks, Ivana," and put it on the floor.

"Is that yours?"

At first I thought she was talking about the gift basket, but she was referring to the copy of *Omni* magazine that was sitting on top of the stack of gifts I'd already opened. *Omni*, a magazine of science and science fiction that had launched in October of that year, was my new obsession. I had just picked up the December issue and brought it with me to the House in the hope that between shrimp cocktail and dinner I'd have a chance to finish reading it.

"Oh, yeah."

"Bob, the publisher, is a friend of mine."

"No way! I love this magazine."

"I'll introduce you. You'll come into the city and meet him."

It wasn't quite as seismic as being told I was going to meet Isaac Asimov, but it was pretty close. "Wow. Thanks."

I filled a plate and went upstairs to my dad's room, where he'd been all day, too sick to join us. He was sitting up, listening to his portable radio. I handed the plate to him, but he put it on the small bedside table, not interested. I told him about Ivana's generous offer.

"Wait a second; *who* does she want to introduce you to?"

I would never forget the name. I'd looked at the magazine's masthead right after speaking to Ivana, and there he was: Bob Guccione, Publisher.

"You're going to meet the guy who publishes *Penthouse*?" Even at thirteen I knew what *Penthouse* was. There was no way we could be talking about the same person. Dad chuckled and said, "I don't think that's such a good idea." And all of a sudden, neither did I.

It was impossible to laugh about the presents my mother received. Why she was still expected to attend family holidays years after her divorce from my father was a mystery, but why she went was an even bigger mystery. Clearly, the Trumps didn't want her there any more than she wanted to be there. Some of the presents they gave her were nice enough, but they always came from lesser stores than the gifts for Ivana and Robert's wife, Blaine. Worse, many of them had clearly been regifted. A handbag she got from Ivana one year bore a luxury brand but contained a used Kleenex.

After dinner and the opening of presents, we split up—some of us went to the kitchen, some to the backyard, and the rest of us to the library, where I sat on the floor near the door with my legs crossed. From a distance I watched whatever Godzilla movie or football game Donald and Rob happened to have on. After a while, I noticed my mother wasn't around. I didn't worry at first, but when she didn't return, I went to look for her. I checked the kitchen but found only my grandmother and aunts. I went out to the backyard, where my brother and David were throwing a football around. When I asked Fritz where she was, he said, "I have no idea," clearly not interested. With time, I would know where to find her without needing to ask, but the first few times I felt panic.

Mom was in the dining room, sitting alone at the table. By then the sideboard had been cleared, and the only evidence of the meal was a few stray cloth napkins on the floor. I stood in the doorway, hoping she would notice me and that my presence would set her back into motion. I was afraid to say anything, not wanting to disturb her. While the clatter of dishes and talk about leftovers and ice cream cake filtered out from the kitchen, I approached the mahogany table in the fading afternoon light. The chandelier had been extinguished, but I wished it had been even darker so that I didn't have to see my mother's face, how stricken she looked.

Careful not to touch her, I sat in the chair next to her. There was no comfort I could give or take except in solidarity.

Eight months before the gift of underwear, Donald and Ivana were married at Marble Collegiate Church and held their reception at the 21 Club. Mom, Fritz, and I were relegated to the cousins' table, and Dad wasn't there. The lie the family told was that Dad had been asked to be Donald's best man and his MC at the reception (a role Joey Bishop actually filled) but the family had decided he needed to stay in Florida in order to take care of Uncle Vic, Gam's brother-in-law. The truth was, my grandfather simply didn't want him at the wedding and he had been told not to come.

While Donald was cruising Manhattan looking for foreclosures, I was losing tens of thousands of dollars almost every week. On Fridays after school, I went to a friend's house and we played our version of Monopoly: double houses and hotels, double the money. Our sessions were marathons spanning the entire weekend. One game could last anywhere from thirty minutes to several hours. The only constant in all of that gaming was my performance: I lost every single time I played.

In order to give me a fighting chance (and my friend something of a challenge), I was allowed to borrow increasingly huge sums of money from the bank and eventually from my opponent. We kept a running total of my enormous debt by writing the sums I owed in long columns of numbers on the inside of the cover.

Despite my terminally poor performance, I never once changed my strategy; I bought every Atlantic City property I landed on and put houses and hotels on my properties even when I had no chance of re-couping my investment. I doubled and tripled down no matter how badly I was losing. It was a great joke between me and my friends that I, the granddaughter and niece of real estate tycoons, was terrible at real es-tate. It turned out that Donald and I had something in common after all.

Since my father's death, Donald has suggested that "they" (meaning he and my grandfather) should have "let" Freddy do what he loved and excelled at (flying) rather than force him to do something he hated and was bad at (real estate). But there's no evidence to suggest that my fa-ther lacked the skills to run Trump Management, just as there is none to suggest that Donald had them.

One night in 1978, Dad woke up in his West Palm Beach apartment with excruciating stomach pains. He managed to drag himself to his car and drove to the emergency room. He later told Mom that when he had gotten to the hospital, he hadn't gone in right away. He had stayed in his car, wondering if he should bother. Perhaps it would be simpler, he had thought, if it just ended. The only thing that had forced him to get help was the thought of me and Fritz.

Dad was very sick and was transferred to a Miami hospital, where the doctors diagnosed him with a heart defect that required surgery. Fred told Maryanne to fly to Florida, get him out of the hospital, and bring him back to New York. It would be my father's last trip north. After three years in Florida, he was going home.

In New York, doctors discovered that Dad had a faulty mitral valve and his heart had become dangerously enlarged. He needed to undergo an experimental procedure to replace it with a healthy valve from a pig's heart.

When Mom and I got to the House to see Dad the day before his surgery, Elizabeth was already there, sitting with him in his tiny childhood bedroom, which we called "the Cell." He lay in his cot, and I kissed him on the cheek but didn't sit next to him for fear of breaking him. I'd seen Dad sick before—with pneumonia, with jaundice, with drunkenness, with despair—but his condition now was shocking. Not yet forty, he looked like a worn-out eighty-year-old man. He told us about the procedure and the pig valve, and Mom said, "Freddy, it's a good thing you're not kosher." We all laughed.

It was a long recovery, and Dad stayed at the House to recuperate. A year after the surgery, he was better than he had been, but he would never be well enough to live on his own again. Part of the obstacle to that may have been financial. He started working for my grandfather again but this time on a maintenance crew. It wasn't surprising that apart from a few stints in rehab to dry out, he had never stopped drinking. He told me once that one of his doctors had warned him, "If you have another drink, it's going to kill you." Even open-heart surgery wasn't enough to stop him.

That Thanksgiving, Dad joined us for the first time since he'd moved back to New York. He sat with me at Gam's end of the table, pale and thin as a specter.

Halfway through the meal, Gam started choking. "You okay, Mom?" Dad asked. Nobody else seemed to notice. As she continued to struggle, a couple of people at the other end of the table looked up to see what was going on but then looked down at their plates and continued eating.

"Come on," Dad said as he put a hand under Gam's elbow and gently helped her to her feet. He led her to the kitchen, where we heard some shuffling and the distressing sound of my grandmother's grunts as Dad performed the Heimlich maneuver; he'd learned it when he had been a volunteer ambulance driver in the late 1960s and early '70s.

When they returned, there was a desultory round of applause. "Good job, Freddy," Rob said, as if my father had just killed a mosquito.

Donald was becoming a constant presence even when he wasn't in the House. Every time my father wanted to go to the kitchen or back to his room, he had to pass through the gauntlet of magazine covers and newspaper articles that littered the breakfast room table. Ever since the 1973 lawsuit, Donald had been a staple of the New York tabloids, and my grandfather had collected every single article that mentioned his name.

The Grand Hyatt deal Donald was working on when Dad moved back to the House was merely a more complex version of the 1972 partnership my grandfather had formed with Donald in New Jersey. The Grand Hyatt was initially made possible because of my grandfather's association with New York City mayor Abe Beame. Fred also contributed generously to both the mayor's and Governor Hugh Carey's campaigns. Louise Sunshine, Carey's fund-raiser, helped pull the deal together. In order to seal it, Beame offered him a $10-million-a-year tax abatement that would remain in place for forty years. When the demolition of the Commodore Hotel began, the New York press, taking Donald at his word, consistently presented the deal as something Donald had accomplished single-handedly.

Perhaps to bridge the gap that had widened between us since he'd moved back to New York, Dad told me he wanted to throw me a Sweet Sixteen party in May 1981. The Grand Hyatt had had its grand opening a few months earlier, and Dad said he'd ask Donald if we could use one of the smaller ballrooms. Donald, who seemed eager for the chance to show off his new project to the family, readily agreed and even offered him a discount.

Dad told my grandfather about the plans for the party a few days later when the three of us were in the breakfast room, the ubiquitous clippings covering the table. "Fred," he said angrily, "Donald's busy, he doesn't need this bullshit."

The subtext was clear: Donald is important, and he's doing important things; you're not.

I don't know how the situation got resolved, but Dad eventually pulled it off. I was going to have my party.

Most of my guests had arrived and I was standing with a small group of friends when Donald made his entrance. He walked over to us, and instead of saying hello, he spread his arms and said, "Isn't this great?"

We all agreed that it was, indeed, great. I thanked him again for letting us use the hotel, then introduced him to everybody.

"So what'd you think of that lobby? Fantastic, right?"

"Fantastic," I said. My friends nodded.

"Nobody else could have pulled this off. Just look at those windows."

I worried that he might tell us how great the bathroom tiles were next, but he saw my grandparents, shook my hand, kissed me on the cheek, said, "Have fun, Honeybunch," and walked over to them. My dad was sitting a couple of tables away from them, by himself.

When I turned back to my friends, they were staring at me.

"What the hell was that?" one of them asked.

In the summer of 1981, Maryanne drove my father to the Carrier Clinic in Belle Mead, New Jersey, about half an hour from the Bedminster property that Donald would later turn into a golf course. Dad went through the thirty-day program, but he did it reluctantly. At the end of his stay, Maryanne and her second husband, John Barry, picked him up and brought him back to the House, arguably the worst place he could be. When she checked on him the next day, Dad had already started drinking again.

Freddy had lost his home and family, his profession, much of his willpower, and most of his friends. Eventually his parents were the only people left to take care of him. And they resented it. In the end, Freddy's very existence infuriated his father.

Fred's treatment of my father had always served as an object lesson to his other children—a warning. In the end, though, the control became something much different. Fred wielded the complete power of the torturer, but he was ultimately as trapped in the circumstance of Freddy's growing dependence due to his alcoholism and declining health as Freddy was tied to him. Fred had no imagination and no ability to see a way beyond the circumstances he was essentially responsible for having created. The situation was proof that his power had limits.

After I got home from summer camp that August, I announced that I wanted to go to boarding school. I explained to Dad that after ten years at Kew-Forest, the same extremely small school my aunts and uncles had gone to, I was feeling hemmed in and bored. I wanted more of a challenge, a place with a campus, better sports facilities, more opportunities. Dad warned me about the dangers of becoming a small fish in a big pond, but I think he understood that although my stated reasons were all true, I also needed to get away.

The problem was that I had only three weeks to figure out where I wanted to go, fill out applications, and get accepted. Over the last two weeks of August 1981, my mother and I visited almost every boarding school in Connecticut and Massachusetts.

While I waited for the results, we needed to get permission from my grandfather, or at least that's what Dad said.

The two of us stood in front of my grandfather's usual spot on the love seat, and Dad explained what I wanted to do. "What does she want to do that for?" my grandfather asked, as if I weren't standing right in front of him. "Kew-Forest is fine." He'd been on the board there for almost thirty years.

"It's just time for a change. Come on, Pop. It'll be good for her."

My grandfather complained about the extra expense, even though the money would come from my father's trust fund and wouldn't affect him at all, and he reiterated his belief in the superiority of Kew-Forest. But Dad didn't back down.

I don't think my grandfather really cared where I went to school, but I was grateful that Dad had stood by my side once again.

The day before heading to boarding school, I left the apartment at the Highlander and rode my bike to my grandparents' house. I coasted down the driveway, propped my bike against the high brick wall next to the garage, then climbed the stairs to the path leading to the back door.

The backyard was quiet in the early-September afternoon. I jumped up the two steps to the cement patio and rang the doorbell. There was no outdoor furniture, just an empty slab. The only person who'd ever used it when we were younger was my uncle Rob. At one time there had been a couple of wrought-iron chairs out there, and when he was home for the weekend, he'd pull them together, and, using one as a footrest, he'd slather himself with baby oil and prop his folding aluminum tanning reflector under his chin.

Minutes passed. I was about to press the doorbell again when my grandmother finally answered the door. She seemed surprised to see me. I pulled the screen door toward me to enter, but Gam remained in the doorway.

"Hi, Gam. I'm here to see Dad."

Gam stood there wiping her hands on her apron, tense, as if I'd just caught her at something. I reminded her that I was leaving for school the next day. She was quite tall, and with her blond hair swept up and pinned tightly behind her head, she looked more severe than usual. She didn't move to let me in.

"Your father's not home," she said. "I don't know when he'll be back."

I was confused. I knew my father had wanted to see me off—we'd talked about it only a few days before. I assumed that he had forgotten I was coming by. In the last year, he'd often forgotten when we had plans. I wasn't surprised, exactly, but something about it still didn't seem right. Directly above where my grandmother and I stood, the sound of a radio came through the open window of my father's bedroom.

I shrugged at Gam, pretending not to care. "Okay, then, I guess tell him to call me later." I moved toward her for a hug, and she put her arms around me stiffly. When I turned to leave, I heard the door close. I walked down the path and down the stairs to the driveway, got on my bike, and rode home. I left for school the next day. Dad never called me.

I was watching a movie in the brand-new auditorium of the Ethel Walker School when the projector went dark and the lights came up. The students were there to watch *The Other Side of the Mountain*, an uplifting story about an Olympic skier who becomes paralyzed in a skiing accident. Instead, *The Other Side of Midnight*—a decidedly different kind of movie with an early rape scene—had been ordered. The faculty were in a bit of a tumult trying to figure out what to do next, while we students thought it was hysterical.

As I sat talking and laughing with some kids from my dorm, I saw Diane Dunn, a phys ed teacher, making her way through the crowd. Dunn was also a counselor at the sailing camp I went to every summer, so I'd known her since I was a little kid. To everyone else at Walker's, she was Miss Dunn, which I found impossible to wrap my head around. At camp she was Dunn and I was Trump, and that's what we continued to call each other. She was largely responsible for my having decided to go to this boarding school, and after I had been there for only two weeks, she was still the only person I really knew.

When she waved me over, I smiled and said, "Hey, Dunn."

"Trump, you need to call home," she said. She had a piece of paper in her fist but didn't give it to me. She looked flustered.

"What's up?"

"You need to call your mother."

"Right now?"

"Yes. If she isn't home, call your grandparents." She was speaking to me as if she'd memorized the lines.

It was almost 10:00 p.m., and I had never called my grandparents so late, but my dad and grandmother were both in the hospital pretty frequently—Dad due to his years of heavy drinking and smoking, and Gam's tendency to break bones fairly often because of her osteoporosis. So I wasn't really worried—or, rather, I didn't think it was anything more serious than usual.

My dorm was adjacent to the auditorium, so I went outside, crossed the oval lawn between them, and climbed the two flights of stairs to my floor. The pay phone hung on the stairwell wall on the landing right next to the door.

I placed a collect call to my mother, but there was no answer, so I dialed the House. Gam answered and accepted the charges—so the emergency wasn't about her. After a quick, muffled "Hello," she immediately handed the phone to my grandfather.

"Yes," he said, brisk and businesslike as usual. For a moment, it was easy to believe that there had been a mistake, that nothing was really wrong. But then something had been urgent enough for me to be pulled out of the auditorium. I had also seen the way Dunn's eyes had widened in panic as she looked for me in the auditorium. It would only occur to me much later that she already knew.

"What's the matter?" I asked.

"Your mother just left," he said. "She should be home in a few minutes." I could picture him in the poorly lit library standing next to the telephone table wearing his starched white shirt, red tie, and navy blue three-piece suit, impatient to be done with me.

"But what's wrong?"

"Your father has been taken to the hospital, but it's nothing to worry about," he said as though reporting the weather.

I could have hung up then. I could have gone back to trying to fit in with my new classmates at my new school.

"Is it his heart?" It was unheard of for me—for anyone but Donald— to challenge my grandfather in any way, but there was obviously a reason I'd been told to call.

"Yes."

"Then it's serious."

"Yes, I would say it's serious." There was a pause during which, per- haps, he was deciding whether to tell me the truth. "Go to sleep," he said finally. "Call your mother in the morning." He hung up.

I stood there in the stairwell with the phone in my hand, not know- ing quite what to do. A door slammed on the floor above me. Footsteps followed, growing louder. A couple of students passed me on their way to the first floor. I put the receiver back into the cradle, picked it up, and tried my mother again.

This time she answered the phone.

"Mom, I just spoke to Grandpa. He told me Dad's in the hospital, but he wouldn't tell me what's going on. Is he okay?"

"He had a heart attack," my mother said.

From the moment she spoke, time took on a different quality. Or maybe it was the next moment, which I don't remember, and the effect of the shock was retroactive. Either way, my mother kept talking but I didn't hear any of the words she said. As far as I could tell, there was no gap in the conversation, but part of it never existed for me.

"He had a heart attack?" I said, echoing the last words I'd heard, as if I hadn't missed something crucial.

"Oh, Mary, he's dead." My mother started to cry. "I really did love him once," she said.

As my mother continued to speak, I slid down the wall until I was sitting on the floor of the landing. I dropped the phone, let it hang on its cord, and waited.

———

Sometime in the afternoon of Saturday, September 26, 1981, one of my grandparents called an ambulance. I didn't know it then, but my father had been critically ill for three weeks. It was the first time anybody had called for medical help.

My grandmother had been a regular at Jamaica Hospital and Booth Memorial Hospital and Medical Center. My dad, too, had been admitted to Jamaica a few times. All of my grandparents' children had been born there, so the family had a long-standing relationship with the staff and administration. My grandparents had donated millions of dollars to Jamaica in particular, and in 1975 the Trump Pavilion for Nursing and Rehabilitation had been named for my grandmother. As for Booth Memorial, my grandmother was heavily involved with the Salvation Army volunteers there—and it was also where I'd spent much of my childhood because of my severe asthma. A single phone call would have guaranteed the best treatment for their son at either facility. No call was made. The ambulance took my father to the Queens Hospital Center in Jamaica. No one went with him.

After the ambulance left, my grandparents called their other four children, but only Donald and Elizabeth could be reached. By the time they arrived in the late afternoon, the information coming from the hospital made it clear that my father's situation was grave. Still nobody went.

Donald called my mother to let her know what was going on but kept getting a busy signal. He got in touch with our superintendent and told him to buzz her on the intercom.

Mom immediately called the House.

"The doctors think Freddy probably won't make it, Linda," Donald told her. My mother had had no idea that Dad was even sick.

"Would it be all right if I came to the House so I can be there if there's any news?" She didn't want to be alone.

When my mother arrived a short time later, my grandparents were sitting alone by the phone in the library; Donald and Elizabeth had gone to the movies.

While Mom sat with my grandparents, nobody said much. A couple of hours later, Donald and Elizabeth returned. When they were told there was no news, Donald left, and Elizabeth, nearing forty, made a cup of tea and went upstairs to her room. As my mother was getting ready to leave, the phone rang. It was the hospital. Dad had been pronounced dead at 9:20 p.m. He was forty-two.

Nobody thought to come get me from school, but arrangements were made for me to take a bus the next morning. Dunn drove me to the Greyhound station in Hartford, where I boarded a bus bound for the Port Authority Bus Terminal in Manhattan. After picking me up in the city, my mother, brother, and I drove to the House, where the rest of the family was already gathered in the breakfast room to discuss the funeral arrangements. Maryanne and her son, my cousin David, were there; my uncle Robert and Blaine; and Donald, Ivana, almost eight months pregnant with Ivanka, and their three-year-old son, Donny. Nobody said much to my mother, brother, or me. There were some attempts at forced heartiness, mostly by Rob, but they didn't land well and soon stopped. My grandfather and Maryanne spoke in hushed tones. My grandmother fretted about what she was going to wear to the wake; my grandfather had picked out a black pantsuit for her, and she wasn't pleased.

In the afternoon, we drove over to R. Stutzmann & Son Funeral Home, a small place in Queens Village about ten minutes from the House, for a private viewing. Before going into the main room, where the coffin was already perched on its stand, I asked my uncle Robert if I could discuss something with him. I pulled him into a small alcove down the hall from the visitation room. "I want to see Dad's body." I saw no reason not to be direct. I didn't have a lot of time.

"You can't, Mary. It's impossible."

"Rob, it's important." It wasn't for religious reasons or because I thought that was how things were done; I had never been to a funeral before and knew nothing about protocol. Although I knew I needed to see my father, I couldn't articulate why. How could I say, "I don't believe he's dead. There's no reason for me to believe that. I didn't even know he was sick"? I could only say, "I need to see him."

Rob paused and finally said, "No, Honeybunch. Your dad is being cremated, and his body hasn't been prepared. It would be terrible for that to be the last memory you have of him."

"It doesn't matter." I felt desperate in a way I didn't understand. Rob looked down at me and then turned to leave. I stepped in front of him. "Please, Rob."

He paused again, then began walking down the hall. "Come on," he said. "We should go in."

On Monday, in between the two sessions of the wake, the family went back to the House for lunch. On the way, Donald and Ivana had gone to the supermarket and picked up large quantities of prepackaged cold cuts that Maryanne and Elizabeth laid out on the breakfast room table and we ate or ignored in relative silence.

I had no appetite and wasn't part of the conversation, so I left the breakfast room to wander around the house, as I'd used to do when I was younger. I walked to the back stairs across from the library doorway and caught a glimpse of Donald holding the telephone in his hand. I don't know if he had just finished a call or was about to make one, but when he noticed me standing in the hallway, he returned the handset to the cradle. Neither one of us spoke. I hadn't seen Donald since Mother's Day, which we had celebrated at North Hills, my grandparents' country club on Long Island. I didn't expect tears from anybody except my grandmother, but Donald, and particularly my grandfather, seemed to be taking my dad's death in stride. "Hey, Donald."

"What's up, Honeybunch?" I sometimes wondered if either of my uncles actually knew my name.

"Dad's going to be cremated, right?" I had known for years that that was what Dad wanted. He had felt so strongly about not being buried that it was one of the first things he had told my mother after they were married. His insistence upon it bordered upon an obsession, which was why I had known about it before I turned ten.

"Right."

"And then what? He's not going to be buried, is he?"

A look of impatience crossed his face. It was clear he didn't want to be having that conversation. "I think he is."

"You know that makes no sense, right?"

"That's what Dad wants." He picked up the phone. When he noticed I wasn't moving, he shrugged and started to dial.

I turned to climb the back stairway. On one end of the long second-floor hallway was Elizabeth's corner room with Maryanne's on the other side of their joint bathroom; on the other, Donald and Robert's shared bedroom was outfitted with blue-and-gold bedspreads and matching window treatments. My grandparents' much larger master bedroom stood right next to theirs and included Gam's separate dressing room with mirrored walls. In the middle of the hallway was the Cell. Dad's cot had been stripped, exposing the thin mattress. His portable radio was still on the small bedside table. The door to the closet was ajar, and I saw a couple of white button-down shirts hanging askew on wire hangers. Even on such a sunny day, the only window let in little light, and the room looked austere in the shadows. I thought I should go in, but there was nothing for me there. I went back downstairs.

The wake fell on the first night of Rosh Hashanah, but many of Dad's fraternity brothers still came. His friend Stu, who had often attended dinner parties and charity events at Jamaica Hospital with his wife, Judy, probably knew my family better than any of Dad's friends other than Billy Drake. Stu saw my grandfather standing alone in the back of the room, and he walked over to pay his respects. The two men shook hands and, after offering his condolences, Stu said, "It looks like real estate isn't doing so well. I hope Donald's okay. I see him in the news a lot, and it looks like he owes the banks a lot of money."

Fred put his arm around his dead son's friend and said with a smile, "Stuart, don't worry about Donald. He's going to be just fine." Donald wasn't there.

My brother gave the only eulogy (or, at least, the only one I remember), written on a sheet of loose-leaf paper, probably on the plane ride from Orlando, where he was a sophomore at Rollins College. He reminisced about the good times he and Dad had had together, most of which had occurred before I had been old enough to remember them, but he refused to shy away from the fundamental reality of my father's life. At one point he referred to Dad as the black sheep of the family, and there were audible gasps from the guests. I felt a thrill of recognition and a sense of vindication—at long last. My brother, who had always been so much better at negotiating the family than I was, had dared tell the truth. I admired his honesty but also felt jealous that he seemed to have so many more good memories of my father than I did.

As the wake drew to a close, I watched as people began to line up, walk past the coffin, pause with eyes closed, hands clasped—sometimes kneeling on a low cushioned bench that seemed to have been put there for the purpose—and then move on.

When my aunt Elizabeth's turn came, she began to sob uncontrollably. In the midst of all that stoicism, her display of emotion was jarring, and people looked at her with muted alarm. But no one approached her. She placed her hands on the coffin and slid to her knees. Her body was shaking so badly that she lost her balance and fell sideways to the floor. I watched her fall. She lay there as if she had no idea where she was or what she was doing and continued to cry. Donald and Robert finally came from the back of the room, where they'd been talking to my grandfather, who stayed where he was.

My uncles lifted Elizabeth from the floor. She limped between them as they pulled her from the room.

I approached the coffin eventually, tentatively. It seemed impossibly small, and I thought that there must have been a mistake. There was no way my father, at six feet two, could have fit inside that box. I ignored the bench and remained on my feet. I bowed my head, concentrating hard on one of the coffin's brass fixtures. Nothing came to me.

"Hi, Dad," I finally said under my breath. I wracked my brains as I stood there looking down, until it occurred to me that I might be standing at the wrong end of the coffin, that the conversation I was trying to have with my father was being directed at his feet. Mortified, I took a step back and returned to my friends.

There was no church ceremony. The coffin was transferred to the crematorium, and we met briefly in the chapel next door—oddly sun-drenched and bright—where a minister of no specified denomination demonstrated both his utter lack of knowledge of my father and the fact that nobody in the family had bothered to educate him about the man he was soon to consign to the flames.

When the business of the funeral was complete, the family planned to take a drive to the All Faiths Cemetery in Middle Village where the family plot was; my grandfather's parents, Friedrich and Elizabeth Trump, were the only occupants at the time. I later learned that over the preceding two days, my mother and my brother and I had separately pleaded with different members of the family to allow my father's ashes to be spread over the waters of the Atlantic Ocean.

Before we left the chapel, I caught up with my grandfather to make one final plea. "Grandpa," I said, "we can't bury Dad's ashes."

"That's not your decision to make."

He started to walk away, but I grabbed his sleeve, knowing it would be my last chance. "Wasn't it his?" I asked. "He wanted to be cremated because he didn't want to be buried. Please, let us take his ashes out to Montauk."

As soon as the words came out of my mouth, I realized that I'd made a critical mistake. My grandfather realized it, too. He associated Montauk with my father's frivolous hobbies, such as boating and fishing, activities that had distracted him from the serious business of real estate.

"Montauk," he repeated, almost smiling. "That's not going to happen. Get in the car."

Sunlight glinted off the marble and granite grave markers as our grandfather, his light blue eyes squinting beneath his enormous eyebrows at the brightness of the day, explained that the tombstone, which was already inscribed with his mother's and father's names, would be removed temporarily so my father's name and dates could be added. As he spoke, he spread his hands wide, like a used-car salesman, bouncing on the balls of his feet, almost jaunty, knowing he was in the presence of a rube.

My grandfather followed the letter of the law and then did what he wanted. After my father was cremated, they put his ashes into a metal box and buried them in the ground.

Dad's death certificate, dated September 29, 1981, states that he died of natural causes. I don't know how that is possible at forty-two. There was no will. If he had anything to leave—books, photographs, his old 78s, his ROTC and National Guard medals—I don't know. My brother got Dad's Timex. I didn't get anything.

The House seemed to grow colder as I got older. The first Thanksgiving after Dad died, the House felt colder still.

After dinner, Rob walked over and put his hand on my shoulder. He pointed to my new cousin, Ivanka, asleep in her crib. "See, that's how it works." I understood the point he was trying to make, but it felt as though it was on the tip of his tongue to say, "Out with the old, in with the new." At least he had tried. Fred and Donald didn't act as if anything was different. Their son and brother was dead, but they discussed New York politics and deals and ugly women, just as they always had.

When Fritz and I were home for Christmas vacation, we met with Irwin Durben, one of my grandfather's lawyers and, after Matthew Tosti died, my mother's main contact, in order to go over the details of my father's estate. I was shocked to find out that he had one. I thought he'd died virtually penniless. But apparently there were trust funds that had been set up by my grandfather and great-grandmother, such as the one that had paid for boarding school, that I didn't know about at the time. They were to be split between me and my brother and kept in trust until we turned thirty. The people appointed to manage those trust funds and to protect our long-term financial interests were Irwin Durben, my aunt Maryanne, and my uncles Donald and Robert. Although Irwin was the point man—it was he we had to call or meet with if we had a question or a problem or any unforeseen financial needs—Donald was the ultimate arbiter of approval and the cosigner of all checks.

Stacks of documents covered Irwin's desk. He sat in his chair behind them and began to explain what, exactly, we were about to sign. Before we got very far, Fritz interrupted him and said, "Mary and I talked about this earlier, and first we need to make sure that Mom will be taken care of."

"Of course," Irwin said. Then over the next two hours he methodically went through every piece of paper. The actual amount of money my father had left wasn't clear to me. The trusts were complex financial arrangements (at least to a sixteen-year-old), and there was what seemed to be a huge tax burden. After explaining each document's significance, Irwin pushed it across the desk for us to sign.

When he finished, he asked if we had any questions.

"No," Fritz said.

I shook my head. I hadn't understood a thing Irwin had said.

PART THREE

Smoke and Mirrors

CHAPTER NINE

The Art of the Bailout

"MARY TRUMP MUGGED" the New York tabloids, subtle as ever, blared in 100-point font the day after Halloween 1991. Even though I already knew what had happened, it was jarring to see the headlines as I passed news kiosks on my way to the subway.

My grandmother hadn't just been mugged, though. The kid who'd grabbed her purse in the grocery store parking lot as she loaded shopping bags into her Rolls-Royce had slammed her head against the car with such force that her brain had hemorrhaged, and she had lost some sight and hearing. When she hit the pavement, her pelvis fractured in several places and ribs broke, injuries that were no doubt more dangerous than they might have been if she hadn't had severe osteoporosis. By the time she arrived at Booth Memorial Hospital, her condition was grave, and we weren't sure if she was going to make it.

It wasn't until she was moved out of the intensive care unit and into a private room that her progress became visible, and it was weeks more before her pain became bearable. When her appetite started to come back, I took her whatever she wanted. One day she was drinking the butterscotch milkshake I'd picked up on the way when Donald showed up.

He said hello to us both and kissed her quickly. "Mom, you look great."

"She's doing much better," I said. He sat in a chair next to the bed and put a foot up on the edge of the bed frame.

"Mary's been visiting me every day," Gam said, smiling at me.

He turned to me. "Must be nice to have so much free time."

I looked at Gam. She rolled her eyes, and I tried not to laugh.

"How are you, sweetheart?" Gam asked him.

"Don't ask." He seemed annoyed.

Gam asked him about his kids, if anything was new with him and Ivana. He didn't have much to say; clearly bored, he left after ten minutes or so. Gam glanced at the door to make sure he was gone. "Somebody's cranky."

Now I did laugh. "To be fair, he's having a tough time," I said. In the last twelve months, the Taj Mahal, his favorite Atlantic City casino, had declared bankruptcy just a little over a year after it had opened; his marriage was a disaster, thanks in part to his very public affair with Marla Maples; the banks had put him on an allowance; and the paperback version of his second book, *Surviving at the Top*, had been published under the title *The Art of Survival*. Despite the fact that he'd brought it all on himself, he seemed put upon rather than humbled or humiliated.

"Poor Donald," Gam mocked. She seemed almost giddy, and I thought the hospital staff might need to cut back on her pain meds. "He was always like this. I shouldn't say it, but when he went to the Military Academy, I was so relieved. He didn't listen to anyone, especially me, and he tormented Robert. And, oh, Mary! He was such a slob. At school he got medals for neatness, then when he came home, he was still a slob!"

"What did you do?"

"What could I do? He never listened to me. And your grandfather didn't care." She shook her head. "Donald got away with murder."

That surprised me. I had always assumed my grandfather was a taskmaster. "That doesn't sound like him."

At the time, my grandfather was at the Hospital for Special Surgery in Manhattan getting a hip replacement. I think he had only ever been in the hospital once, when he'd had a tumor on his neck near his right ear removed in 1989. I don't know if the timing of his hip surgery was a coincidence or if it had been scheduled after Gam was admitted so she wouldn't have to deal with him while she recovered. His mental state had been deteriorating for some time and while he was in the hospital had definitely taken a turn for the worse. A few times, late at night, the nurses found him trying to leave wearing only boxer shorts. He told them he was going to find Mrs. Trump. Gam seemed pretty happy not to be found.

Donald's perceived success with the Grand Hyatt in 1980 had paved the way for Trump Tower, which had opened to great fanfare in 1983. From his reportedly abysmal treatment of the undocumented workers who built it to the alleged Mob involvement, the project was steeped in controversy. The affronts culminated in the destruction of the beautiful Art Deco limestone reliefs on the facade of the Bonwit Teller building, which he razed to make room for his. Donald had promised those historically significant artifacts to the Metropolitan Museum of Art. Realizing that removing them in one piece would cost money and slow down construction, he instead ordered that they be destroyed. When confronted with that breach of trust and taste, he shrugged it off, declaring the sculptures to be "without artistic merit," as if he knew better than the considered assessment of experts. Over time that attitude—that he knew better—would become even more entrenched: as his knowledge base has decreased (particularly in areas of governing), his claims to know everything have increased in direct proportion to his insecurity, which is where we are now.

The real reason Donald's first two projects were acquired and developed relatively smoothly was in large part because of Fred's expertise as a developer and dealmaker. Neither would have been possible without his contacts, influence, approval, money, knowledge, and, maybe most important, endorsement of Donald.

Before that point, Donald had relied entirely on Fred's money and influence—although he never acknowledged it and publicly credited his own wealth and savvy for his success. The media were more than happy to go along without question, and the banks followed suit when Donald started to pursue the idea of becoming a casino operator in New Jersey, which in 1977 had legalized gambling in Atlantic City in an effort to save the flailing seaside resort town. If my grandfather's opinion had carried any weight with him, Donald would never have invested in Atlantic City. Manhattan was worth the risk, as far as Fred was concerned, but in Atlantic City he would have nothing except money and advice to offer—no political clout or knowledge of the industry to draw on. By then Fred's influence over him was waning, and in 1982 Donald applied for his gaming license.

While her brother was casting about for investment opportunities, Maryanne, who had been an assistant district attorney in New Jersey since the mid-1970s, asked Donald if he would ask Roy Cohn to do him a favor. Cohn had enough clout with the Reagan administration that he was given access to AZT, an experimental AIDS treatment, as well as influence over judicial appointments. Conveniently, a seat was open in the US District Court for the District of New Jersey. Maryanne thought it would be a great fit, and Donald thought it might be useful to have a close relative on the bench in a state in which he planned to do a lot of business. Cohn gave Attorney General Ed Meese a call, and Maryanne was nominated in September and confirmed in October.

In yet another sign of Fred's waning influence, Donald had purchased a $300 million–plus casino that would become Trump's Castle sight unseen in 1985, only a year after he had bought Harrah's, which became Trump Plaza. For Donald, too much of a good thing was a better thing; Atlantic City had unlimited potential, he believed, so two casinos were better than one. By then Donald's ventures already carried billions of dollars of debt (by 1990, his personal obligation would balloon to $975 million). Even so, that same year he bought Mar-a-Lago for $8 million. In 1988, he'd bought a yacht for $29 million and then, in 1989, the Eastern Air Lines Shuttle for $365 million. In 1990, he'd had to issue almost $700 million in junk bonds, carrying a 14 percent interest rate, just to finish construction on his third casino, the Taj Mahal. It seemed as if the sheer volume of purchases, the price tags of the acquisitions, and the audacity of the transactions kept everybody, including the banks, from paying attention to his fast-accumulating debt and questionable business acumen.

Back then, Donald's favorite color scheme was red, black, and gold, so Atlantic City's cheap glitz appealed to him almost as much as the allure of easy money. The house always wins, after all, and it was a good bet that anybody who could afford the buy-in would do well there. Atlantic City was completely outside of Fred's purview, which also appealed to Donald. Setting aside the massive monetary investments made by Fred and others, operating a casino, unlike the Grand Hyatt and Trump Tower, which were development projects that were ultimately managed by other entities, would be an ongoing business. As such, it would have been Donald's first opportunity to succeed independently of his father.

Having his own casino provided Donald an outsize canvas; he could tailor that entire world to his specifications. And if one casino was good, two would be better and three even better than that. Of course, his casinos were competing with one another and eventually would be cannibalizing one another's profits. As absurd as it was, there was a certain logic to his wanting more—after all, it had worked for his father. But Donald didn't understand, and refused to learn, that owning and running casinos were vastly different from owning and running rental properties in Brooklyn, from the business model and the market to the customer base and the calculus involved. Because he couldn't see that glaring distinction, it was easy for him to believe that more was better in Atlantic City, just as it had been for my grandfather in New York's outer boroughs. If one casino was a cash cow, three would be a herd of them. He would do with casinos what Fred had done with his apartment buildings.

The only part of the scenario that defies explanation is the fact that the banks and investors in his first two casinos didn't object more strenuously to his opening a third, which would cut into their own bottom lines. It made even less sense that he could find anybody interested in investing in it. Even a casual glance at the numbers—not least, the debt service—should have scared the most reckless lender away. In the late 1980s, nobody said no to Donald, thereby legitimizing another misguided project that had the ancillary benefit of bolstering the ego of a man who had no way of making it succeed.

In August of that year, *Surviving at the Top* was published, and within weeks it would become clear that the book's subject matter and timing were bad enough to qualify as parody.

In June 1990, Donald missed a $43 million payment for Trump's Castle. Six months later, my grandfather sent his chauffeur with more than $3 million in cash to purchase chips at the Castle. In other words, he bought the chips with no intention of gambling with them; his driver simply put them in a briefcase and left the casino. Even that wasn't enough. The next day, my grandfather wired another $150,000 to the Castle, presumably for more chips. Although those maneuvers helped temporarily, they resulted in my grandfather's having to pay a $30,000 fine for violating a gaming commission rule prohibiting unauthorized financial sources from lending money to casinos. If he wanted to continue lending Donald money to keep his casinos afloat (which he did), he would also be required to get a gaming license in New Jersey. But it was too late. Donald might have controlled 30 percent of Atlantic City's market share, but the Taj was making it impossible for his two other casinos to make money (the Plaza and Castle lost a combined $58 million the year the Taj opened), the three properties carried $94 million in annual debt, and the Taj alone needed to pull in *more than $1 million a day* to break even.

The banks were bleeding money. Just as the Taj was opening, Donald and his lenders were meeting to try to figure out how to rein in and manage his spending. The possibility of more defaults and bankruptcies still loomed, and a solution had to be found that would protect Donald's image, which, in turn, would protect the banks' money.

Without the veneer of success and confidence he projected (and had projected for him), the bankers feared that his properties, already in trouble, would lose even more value. His last name was the draw: without the name there would be no new gamblers or tenants or people willing to buy bonds and hence no new revenue.

In addition to fronting Donald the money to cover his businesses' operating expenses, the banks reached an agreement with him in May 1990 to put him on a $450,000-a-month allowance—that is, almost $5.5 million a year for having failed miserably. That money was just for personal expenses: the Trump Tower triplex apartment, the private jet, the mortgage on Mar-a-Lago. In order to sell his image, Donald needed to be able to continue living the lifestyle that bolstered it.

In order for the banks to keep tabs on him, Donald had to meet with them every Friday to report on his expenditures as well as progress he'd made selling assets such as the yacht. In May 1990, there was no denying how dire the situation was. As much as Donald complained to Robert that the banks were "killing" him, the truth was that he was beholden to them in a way he had never been to his father: he had never been on a leash before, let alone a short one, and it chafed. He was legally obligated to pay the banks back, and if he didn't, there would be consequences. At least there should have been.

Despite the restrictions, Donald continued spending cash he didn't have, including $250,000 for Marla's engagement ring and $10 million to Ivana as part of their divorce settlement. I don't think it ever occurred to him that he couldn't spend whatever he wanted no matter what the circumstances. The banks admonished him for betraying their agreement, but they never took any action against him, which just reinforced his belief that he could do whatever he wanted, as he almost always had.

In a way, you can't really blame Donald. In Atlantic City, he had become unmoored from his need for his father's approval or permission. He no longer needed to talk himself up; his exaggerated assessment of himself was simultaneously fueled and validated by banks that were

throwing hundreds of millions of dollars at him and a media that lav-
ished him with attention and unwarranted praise. The two combined
rendered him blind to how dire his situation was. My grandfather's
myths about Donald were now being reinforced by the world at large.

Regardless of who was disseminating them, however, they were still
myths. Donald was, in essence, still Fred's construct. Now he belonged
to the banks and the media. He was both enabled by and dependent
upon them, just as he had been upon Fred. He had a streak of superficial charm, even charisma, that sucked certain people in. When his
ability to charm hit a wall, he deployed another "business strategy":
throwing tantrums during which he threatened to bankrupt or otherwise ruin anybody who failed to let him have what he wanted. Either
way, he won.

Donald was successful because he was a success. That was a premise
that ignored one fundamental reality: he had not achieved and could
not achieve what he was being credited with. Despite that, his ego, now
unleashed, had to be fed continually, not just by his family but by all
who encountered it.

New York's elite would never accept him as anything but the court
jester from Queens, but they also validated his pretensions and grandi-
ose self-image by inviting him to their parties and allowing him to frequent their haunts (such as Le Club). The more New Yorkers wanted
spectacle, the more willing the media were to provide it—even at the
expense of more important and substantive stories. Why bore them
with hard-to-follow articles about his convoluted bank transactions?
The distractions and sleights of hand benefited Donald enormously
while giving him exactly what he wanted: the ongoing adulation of
media that focused on his salacious divorce and alleged sexual prow-
ess. If the media could deny reality, so could he.

By some miracle, I had gotten into Tufts University after boarding
school, and despite dropping out the second semester of my freshman
year, I graduated in 1989. A year later, just before my grandfather's

modest purchase of $3.15 million worth of casino chips, I entered the graduate program in English and comparative literature at Columbia University.

Two months after the semester started, my apartment was burgled. All of my electronics, including my typewriter, which was essential for school, were taken. When I called Irwin to see if I could get an advance on my allowance, he refused. My grandfather thought I should get a job, he told me.

The next time I visited my grandmother at the House, I explained the situation to her, and she offered to write me a check. "It's okay, Gam. I only have to wait a couple of weeks."

"Mary," she said, "never reject a gift of money." She wrote me the check, and I was able to buy a typewriter later that week.

I soon got an angry call from Irwin. "Did you ask your grandmother for money?"

"Not exactly," I said. "I told her I got robbed, and she helped me out."

While going through the canceled checks of all of his personal and business accounts, as well as my grandmother's, as he did at the end of every month, my grandfather had discovered the check my grandmother had written to me, and he was furious.

"You need to be careful," Irwin warned me. "Your grandfather often speaks of disowning you."

I got another call from Irwin a few weeks later. My grandfather was angry with me again, this time because he didn't like the signature with which I endorsed my checks.

"Irwin, you've got to be kidding."

"I'm not. He hates the fact that it's illegible."

"It's a *signature*."

He paused and softened his tone. "Change it. Mary, you've got to play the game. Your grandfather thinks you're being selfish, and there may be nothing left by the time you turn thirty." But I never understood what he meant by "the game"—it was my family, not a bureaucracy.

"I don't see what I'm doing wrong. I'm getting a master's degree at an Ivy League university."

"He doesn't care."

"Does Donald know about this?"

"Yes."

"He's my trustee. What does he have to say?"

"Donald?" Irwin laughed dismissively. "Nothing."

My grandfather hadn't yet been diagnosed with Alzheimer's disease, but he'd been struggling with dementia for a while by then, so I didn't take the threats too seriously. I did, however, change my signature.

Everyone in my family experienced a strange combination of privilege and neglect. Although I had all of the material things I needed—and luxuries such as private schools and summer camp—there was a purposely built-in idea of uncertainty that any of it would last. By the same token, there was the sometimes dispiriting and sometimes devastating sense that nothing any of us did really mattered or, worse, that *we* didn't matter—only Donald did.

Trump Management, which Donald often referred to as a "two-bit operation," was doing fairly well. Fred paid himself more than $109 million between 1988 and 1993 and had tens of millions more in the bank. The Trump Organization, the company Donald ostensibly ran, was, however, in increasingly serious trouble.

Reduced to a monthly allowance—that a family of four could have lived on comfortably for ten years but still an allowance—and shut out by the banks, which finally refused to lend him more money, Donald fully believed that whatever was happening to him was the result of the economy, the poor treatment he received from the banks, and bad luck.

Nothing was ever fair to him. That struck a chord in Fred, who nursed his own grievances and also never took responsibility for anything other than his successes. Donald's talent for deflecting responsibility while projecting blame onto others came straight from his father's playbook. Even with the untold millions of dollars Fred spent, he couldn't prevent Donald's failures, but he could certainly find a scapegoat, just as he had always done when his missteps and poor judgment caught up with him, as when he blamed Freddy for the failure of Steeplechase. Donald knew that taking responsibility for your failures, which obviously meant acknowledging failure, was not something Fred admired; he'd seen where it had gotten Freddy.

It's very possible that back in the late 1960s and early '70s, Fred didn't know just how deep Donald's ineptitude ran. Acknowledging weakness of any kind in the son on whom he had staked the future of his empire and for whom he had sacrificed Freddy would have been nearly impossible. It was much easier to convince himself that Donald's talents were wasted in the backwater of Brooklyn; he simply needed a bigger pond in which to make a splash.

As the Commodore Hotel slowly transformed into the Grand Hyatt, Fred was so blinded by the success with which Donald manipulated and debased every part of the process in order to get his way that he seemed to forget how vital his own connections, knowledge, and skills were; neither the Hyatt nor Trump Tower would have seen the light of day without them. Even Fred's head must have been turned by all of the attention Donald generated for two projects that, if developed by anybody else, would have been considered fairly commonplace occurrences in Manhattan.

Fred had known all along what games Donald was playing, because he'd taught Donald how to play them. Working the refs, lying, cheating—as far as Fred was concerned, those were all legitimate business tactics. The most effective game for both father and son was the shell game. While Fred kept churning out projects and solidifying his status as a "postwar master builder," he was fattening his wallet with taxpayer money by skimming off the top and allegedly committing so much tax fraud that four of his children would continue to benefit from it for decades. While the rubes focused on the salacious details Donald kept generating for the tabloids, he was building a reputation for success based on bad loans, bad investments, and worse judgment. The difference between the two, however, is that despite his dishonesty and lack of integrity, Fred actually ran a solid, income-generating business, while Donald had only his ability to spin and his father's money to prop up an illusion.

Once Donald moved into Atlantic City, there was no longer any denying that he wasn't just ill-suited to the day-to-day grind of running a few dozen middle-class rental properties in the outer boroughs, he was ill-suited to running any kind of business at all—even one that ostensibly played to his strengths of self-promotion and self-aggrandizement and his taste for glitz.

When Fred bragged about Donald's brilliance and claimed that his son's success had far outpaced his own, he must have known that not a word of it was true; he was too smart and too good at arithmetic to think otherwise: the numbers simply didn't add up. But the fact that Fred continued to prop Donald up despite the wisdom of continuing to do so suggests that something else was going on.

Because Fred did deny the reality on the ground in Atlantic City. He had already shown himself impervious to facts that didn't fit his narrative, so he blamed the banks and the economy and the casino industry just as vociferously as his son did. Fred had become so invested in the fantasy of Donald's success that he and Donald were inextricably linked. Facing reality would have required acknowledging his own responsibility, which he would never do. He had gone all in, and although any rational person would have folded, Fred was determined to double down.

There was still plenty of publicity to turn Fred's head, and thanks to the banks that father and son maligned, the extraordinary financial reversal didn't put a dent in Donald's lifestyle. Finally, there was the slow-rolling toll that his as-yet-undiagnosed Alzheimer's was beginning to take on his executive functioning. Already susceptible to believing the best of his worst son, it became easier over time for him to confuse the hype about Donald with reality.

As usual, the lesson Donald learned was the one that supported his preexisting assumption: no matter what happens, no matter how much damage he leaves in his wake, *he* will be okay. Knowing ahead of time that you're going to be bailed out if you fail renders the narrative leading up to that moment meaningless. Claim that a failure is a tremendous victory, and the shameless grandiosity will retroactively make it so. That guaranteed that Donald would never change, even if he were capable of changing, because he simply didn't need to. It also guaranteed a cascade of increasingly consequential failures that would ultimately render all of us collateral damage.

As the bankruptcies and embarrassments mounted, Donald was confronted for the first time with the limits of his ability to talk or threaten his way out of a problem. Always adept at finding an escape hatch, he seems to have come up with a plan to betray his father and steal vast sums of money from his siblings. He secretly approached two of my grandfather's longest-serving employees, Irwin Durben, his lawyer, and Jack Mitnick, his accountant, and enlisted them to draft a codicil to my grandfather's will that would put Donald in complete control of Fred's estate, including the empire and all its holdings, after he died. Maryanne, Elizabeth, and Robert would effectively be at Donald's financial mercy, dependent on his approval for the smallest transaction.

As Gam later told Maryanne, when Irwin and Jack went to the House to have Fred sign the codicil, they presented the document as if it had been Fred's idea all along. My grandfather, who was having one of his more lucid days, sensed that something was not right, although he couldn't say exactly what. He angrily refused to sign. After Irwin and Jack left, Fred conveyed his concerns to his wife. My grandmother immediately called her oldest child to explain what had happened as best she could. In short, she said, "it simply didn't pass the smell test."

Maryanne, with her background as a prosecutor, had limited knowledge of trusts and estates. She asked her husband, John Barry, a well-known and respected attorney in New Jersey, to recommend someone who could help, and he asked one of his colleagues to look into the situation. It didn't take long for Donald's scheme to be uncovered. As a result, my grandfather's entire will was rewritten, replacing one he had written in 1984, and Maryanne, Donald, and Robert were all named as executors. In addition, a new standard was put into place: whatever Fred gave Donald, he would have to give an equal amount to each of the other three children.

Maryanne would say years later, "We would have been penniless. Elizabeth would have been begging on a street corner. We would have had to beg Donald if we wanted a cup of coffee." It was "sheer luck" that they had stopped the scheme. Yet the siblings still got together every holiday as though nothing had happened.

Donald's attempt to wrest control of Fred's estate away from him was the logical outcome of Fred's leading his son to believe that he was the only person who mattered. Donald had been given more of everything; he had been *invested* in; elevated to the detriment of Maryanne, Elizabeth, and Robert (and even his mother) and at the expense of Freddy. In Donald's mind, the success and reputation of the entire family rested on his shoulders. Given that, it makes sense in the end that he would feel he deserved not just more than his fair share but everything.

I was standing at the window of my studio apartment looking at the rush-hour traffic clogging the 59th Street Bridge when Donald called me from his plane, not a usual occurrence.

"The dean of students at Tufts sent me a letter you wrote."

"Really? Why?"

It took me a minute to realize what he was talking about. One of my professors had been up for tenure, and before I graduated, I had written a letter in support of him. That had been four years earlier, and I'd forgotten all about it.

"The letter was to show me how great you thought Tufts was. It was a fund-raising thing."

"I'm sorry. That was rude of him."

"No, it's a fantastic letter."

The point of the conversation was eluding me. Then Donald said, apropos of nothing as far as I could tell, "Do you want to write my next book? The publisher wants me to get started, and I thought it would be a great opportunity for you. It'll be fun."

"That sounds incredible," I said. And it did. I heard the plane engine rev in the background and remembered where he was. "Where are you going, anyway?"

"Heading back from Vegas. Call Rhona tomorrow." Rhona Graff was his executive assistant at the Trump Organization.

"I will. Thanks, Donald."

It wasn't until later, when I reread the letter, that I understood why Donald thought it would be a good idea to hire me—not because it was "fantastic" but because it demonstrated that I was really good at making other people look really good.

A few days later, I was given my own desk in the back office of the Trump Organization. A nondescript, open space with drop ceilings, fluorescent lighting, and huge steel filing cabinets lining the walls, it had a lot more in common with the utilitarian office of Trump Management on Avenue Z than the gold-and-glass walls lined with magazine covers featuring Donald's face that greeted guests out front.

I spent the first week on the job familiarizing myself with the people who worked there and the filing system. (To my surprise, there was a folder with my name on it containing a single sheet of paper—a handwritten letter I had sent to Donald my junior year in high school. I'd asked if he could get me a pair of tickets to a Rolling Stones concert. He couldn't.) I kept to myself for the most part, but whenever I had a question, Ernie East, one of Donald's vice presidents and a very nice man, helped me out. He suggested documents that might be useful, and on occasion he'd put some file folders on my desk that he thought might help. The problem was that I didn't really know what the book was supposed to be about beyond its broad theme, which I cleverly deduced from its working title, *The Art of the Comeback*.

I hadn't read either of Donald's other two books, but I knew a bit about them. *The Art of the Deal*, as far as I understood it, had been meant to present Donald as a serious real estate developer. The book's ghostwriter, Tony Schwartz, had done a good job—which he has long since regretted—of making his subject sound coherent, as if Donald had actually espoused a fully realized business philosophy that he understood and lived by.

After the embarrassment of the poorly timed publication of *Surviving at the Top*, I assumed that Donald wanted a return to the relative seriousness of its predecessor. I set about trying to explain how, under the most adverse circumstances, he had emerged from the depths, victorious and more successful than he had ever been. There wasn't much evidence to support that narrative—he was about to experience his fourth bankruptcy filing with the Plaza Hotel—but I had to try.

Every morning on the way to my desk, I stopped by to see Donald in the hope that he'd have time to sit down with me for an interview. I figured that would be the best way to find out what he had done and how he had done it. His perspective was everything, and I needed the stories in his own words. He was usually on a call, which he'd put on speaker as soon as I sat down. The calls, as far as I could tell, were almost never about business. The person on the other end, who had no idea he or she was on speaker, was looking for gossip or for Donald's opinion about women or a new club that had opened. Sometimes he was being asked for a favor. Often the conversation was about golf. Whenever anything outrageously sycophantic, salacious, or stupid was said, Donald smirked and pointed to the speakerphone as if to say, "What an idiot."

When he wasn't on a call, I'd find him going through the newspaper clippings that were collected for him daily. Every article was about him or at least mentioned him. He showed them to me, something he did with most visitors. Depending on the content of the article, he sometimes wrote on it with a blue Flair felt-tip marker, just like the one my grandfather used, and sent it back to the reporter. After he finished writing, he'd hold up the clipping and ask for my opinion of what he considered his witty remarks. That did not help me with my research.

A few weeks after Donald hired me, I still hadn't gotten paid. When I brought it up to him, he pretended at first not to understand what I was talking about. I pointed out that I needed an advance so I could at least buy a computer and a printer—I was still writing on the same electric typewriter I'd bought with Gam's help in grad school. He said he thought that was the publisher's problem. "Can you talk to Random House?"

I didn't realize it at the time, but Donald's editor had no idea he'd hired me.

One night, as I sat at home trying to figure out how to piece together something vaguely interesting out of the uninteresting documents I'd been poring over, Donald called. "When you come to the office to-morrow, Rhona's going to have some pages for you. I've been working on material for the book. It's really good." He sounded excited.

Finally I might have something to work with, some idea about how to organize this thing. I still didn't know what he thought about his "comeback," how he ran his business, or even what role he played in the deals he was currently developing.

The next day, Rhona handed me a manila envelope containing about ten typewritten pages, as promised. I took it to my desk and began to read. When I finished, I wasn't sure what to think. It was clearly a transcript of a recording Donald had made, which explained its stream-of-consciousness quality. It was an aggrieved compendium of women he had expected to date but who, having refused him, were suddenly the worst, ugliest, and fattest slobs he'd ever met. The biggest takeaways were that Madonna chewed gum in a way Donald found un-attractive and that Katarina Witt, a German Olympic figure skater who had won two gold medals and four world championships, had big calves.

I stopped asking him for an interview.

———

From time to time, Donald asked about my mother. He hadn't seen her in four years, ever since Ivana and Blaine had given Gam an ultimatum just before Thanksgiving: either Linda came to the House for the holidays, or they did. They found their not-exactly sister-in-law too quiet and depressed, and they just couldn't have a good time with her there. My mother had been in the Trump family since 1961, and though I never understood why my grandfather required her presence at holidays after my parents divorced, she always went. More than twenty-five years later, my grandmother chose Ivana and Blaine, without factoring in how the decision might affect me and my brother.

Now Donald said, "I think we made a big mistake continuing to support your mother. It might have been better if we'd cut her off after a couple of years and she had to stand on her own two feet."

The idea that anyone else was entitled to money or support he or she wasn't obviously earning was impossible for Donald and my grandfather to fathom. Nothing my mother had received as the former wife of the oldest son of a very wealthy family, who had raised two of Fred and Mary Trump's grandchildren almost single-handedly, had come from my grandfather, and it *certainly* hadn't come from Donald, yet they both acted as if it did.

Donald probably thought he was being kind. There used to be a spark of that in him. He did once give me $100 to get my car out of impound. And after my father died, Donald was the only member of my family, other than my grandmother, who included me in anything. But his kindness had become so warped over time—through lack of use and Fred's discouragement—that what he considered kindness would have been practically unrecognizable to the rest of us. I didn't know it at the time, but when we had that conversation, Donald was still receiving his $450,000 allowance from the banks every month.

One morning as I sat across from Donald at his desk going over the details of our trip to Mar-a-Lago (Donald thought it would help me with the book if I saw his Palm Beach mansion firsthand) the phone rang. It was Philip Johnson.

As they chatted, Donald suddenly seemed to get an idea. He put the phone on speaker. "Philip!" he said. "You have to talk to my niece. She's writing my next book. You can tell her all about the Taj."

I introduced myself, and Philip suggested I come to his house in Connecticut the following week to discuss the book.

After Donald finished the call, he said to me, "That'll be fantastic. Philip is a great guy. I hired him to design the porta-co-share for the Taj Mahal. It's tremendous—I'd never seen anything like it."

After we finished discussing the logistics of our trip to Florida, I left the office and headed to the library. I had no idea who Philip Johnson was, and I'd never heard of a "porta-co-share."

In the limo on the way to the airport the following day, I told Donald that I'd arranged to meet Johnson at his home, which I'd learned at the library was the very famous Glass House that he, a very famous architect, had designed. I had also discovered that the thing Johnson had designed for the Taj—what Donald called a porta-co-share—was a porte cochere, basically a large carport. I understood why Donald had wanted Johnson to be involved in the project; he wasn't just famous, he also traveled in the kind of circles Donald aspired to. I didn't, however, understand why Johnson would bother designing the Taj's carport. It was a very small-scale project that seemed not worth his while.

When Donald picked up a copy of the *New York Post* less than ten minutes into the car ride, I knew he had no intention of giving me information for the book. I'd begun to suspect that he'd hired me without consulting his publisher because he didn't want to be micromanaged by the people there. It would also be a lot easier to put off his niece, who wasn't under contract and was barely getting paid, than a professional writer, who would most likely have a significant stake in the success of the book. But we were about to be trapped together on a plane for two hours, so I hoped he might talk to me then.

When we got into the cabin of the jet that was waiting for us on the tarmac, Donald spread out his arms and asked, "So what do you think?"

"It's great, Donald." I knew the drill.

As soon as we reached cruising altitude and we could unbuckle our seat belts, one of his bodyguards handed him a huge stack of mail after setting a glass of Diet Coke next to him. I watched as he opened one envelope after another, then, after examining the contents for a few seconds, threw them and the envelope onto the floor. When a large pile accumulated, the same guy would reappear, pick up the wastepaper, and throw it into the garbage. That happened over and over again. I moved to another seat so I didn't have to watch.

The staff were waiting as the car pulled up to the entrance at Mar-a-Lago. Donald went off with his butler, and I introduced myself to everybody else. The fifty-eight-bedroom mansion with thirty-three bathrooms outfitted with fixtures plated in gold and an eighteen-hundred-square-foot living room that sported forty-two-foot ceilings was as garish and uncomfortable as I'd expected.

Dinner that evening was just me, Donald, and Marla. She and I had met a few times before, but we had never had a chance to get to know each other one on one. I found her friendly, and Donald seemed relaxed with her. She was just two years older than I was and about as different from Ivana as a human being could be. Marla was down to earth and soft spoken where Ivana was all flash, arrogance, and spite.

The next day, I spent the morning exploring the property. There were no other guests, so the entire place felt empty and strangely quiet. I talked to the butler to see if he had any interesting stories, got to know some of the other guys who worked there, and then took a quick swim before lunch, which was scheduled for 1:00 p.m. As formal as Mar-a-Lago was in some ways, it was also much more casual than our usual family gathering places, so I felt comfortable wearing a bathing suit and a pair of shorts to lunch, which was being served on the patio.

Donald, who was wearing golf clothes, looked up at me as I approached as if he'd never really seen me before. "Holy shit, Mary. You're stacked."

"Donald!" Marla said in mock horror, slapping him lightly on the arm.

I was twenty-nine and not easily embarrassed, but my face reddened, and I suddenly felt self-conscious. I pulled my towel around my shoulders. It occurred to me that nobody in my family, outside of my parents and brother, had ever seen me in a bathing suit. Unfortunately for the book, that was about the only interesting thing that happened during my entire visit to Palm Beach.

Back in New York, Donald finally got sick of my asking him to sit for an interview and handed me a list of names. "Talk to these people." Included were the presidents of his casinos and Maryanne's husband, John. Although that was potentially helpful, he didn't seem to understand that writing the book without any input from him would be close to impossible.

I met with all the presidents of the casinos. Not surprisingly, a lot of their answers were canned, and I realized that they weren't going to give me dirt on what was happening in their boss's business at the height of the chaos and dysfunction. The trips weren't a total waste of time; I'd never been down there before, and at least I got a sense of the place.

My meeting with John Barry was even less productive than the trips to Atlantic City.

"What can you tell me?" I asked him.

He rolled his eyes.

Finally Donald told me his editor wanted to meet with me. A lunch was set up, and I arrived at the restaurant thinking he and I were going to be discussing next steps. It was an expensive "in" place in Midtown, and we were seated at a small, cramped table near the kitchen.

With very little preliminary conversation, the editor told me that

Random House wanted Donald to hire someone with more experience.

"I've been working on this for a while," I said, "and I think I've made some progress. The problem is, I can't get Donald to sit down with me for an interview."

"You can't expect to play a Mozart concerto the first time you sit down at a piano," the editor said, as if I'd just learned the alphabet the day before.

"Donald told me he likes what I've done so far," I said.

The editor looked at me as if I'd just proved his point for him. "Donald hasn't read any of it," he said.

I stopped at the office the next day to clear out my desk and hand over anything that might be useful to my eventual replacement. I wasn't upset. I didn't even mind that Donald had had somebody else fire me. The project had hit a wall. Besides, after all of the time I had spent in his office, I still had no idea what he actually did.

CHAPTER TEN

Nightfall Does Not Come at Once

We were sitting at the same table at Mar-a-Lago where I'd had lunch with Donald and Marla a couple of years earlier. The family had started going there for Easter. My grandfather turned to my grandmother, pointed to me, smiled, and asked, "Who is this nice lady?"

He turned to me. "Aren't you a nice lady."

"Thank you, Grandpa," I said.

Gam seemed upset. I told her not to worry. I'd already seen people my grandfather had known for decades erased from his memory: his youngest grandchildren, his driver. His new nickname for me stuck, and he called me "nice lady" until his final illness. He said it gently and with apparent kindness; he was very sweet to me after he'd forgotten who I was.

"Come on, Pop." Rob took a step, but my grandfather didn't move. He looked around at the crowds of people at a gala thrown in my grandparents' honor, and his eyes glazed over with a look of sheer panic, as if he suddenly had no idea who anybody was or what he was doing there. Up until then, I had only seen my grandfather look contemptuous, annoyed, angry, amused, and self-satisfied. The look of fear was new and alarming. The only other time I had seen my grandfather look unsettled at all was on the one occasion Donald had taken him to play golf—a hobby that Donald spent an inordinate amount of time on but that Fred, who had no use for pastimes, never complained about. I was at the House when they came back from the course, and I almost didn't recognize him. They were both wearing golf clothes—my grandfather in light blue pants, a white cardigan, and matching white shoes. It was the first time I'd ever seen my grandfather wearing something other than a suit. I'd never seen him look so uncomfortable and self-conscious before.

Soon he'd go from habitually misplacing things and forgetting a word or a conversation here and there to forgetting familiar faces. You could measure your worth in my grandfather's eyes by how long he remembered you. I don't know if he remembered Dad, because I never once heard him mention my father in the years after his death.

Maryanne made sure my cousin David, by then a clinical psychologist, accompanied my grandfather to all of his appointments for checkups and neurological exams in a concerted effort to cement him in my grandfather's memory, but it didn't take long before my grandfather simply referred to David as "the doctor."

I was standing with Maryanne and my grandfather by the pool at Mar-a-Lago when he pointed to me and said to his daughter, "Isn't she a nice lady?" A year or so had passed since he'd first given me the sobriquet.

"Yes, Dad," Maryanne said. She smiled wearily.

He looked at her carefully and, almost as an afterthought, asked, "Who are you?"

Her eyes watered as if somebody had slapped her. "Dad," she said gently, "it's Maryanne."

"Okay, Maryanne." He smiled, but the name didn't mean anything to him anymore.

He never forgot Donald.

Rob, who'd left his position as president of Trump's Castle (of the infamous $3.15 million chip bailout) under a cloud, had sat in for my grandfather at Trump Management during his 1991 hospitalization and never left. It was a good gig for Robert. In addition to the millions of dollars a year he got simply by virtue of the fact that he was one of Fred's living children, he was also paid half a million dollars a year to do a job that required little skill or effort. It was the position for which Freddy and then Donald had been groomed—and had rejected, each in his own way.

Fred still went to the office every day and sat behind his desk until it was time to go home, but Rob was actually, if not nominally, in charge of the well-oiled, self-sustaining machine he often referred to as a "cash cow."

My grandfather was having a bad day. Most of us were gathered in the library when he came down the stairs, his mustache and eyebrows freshly dyed and his wig askew but impeccably dressed in his three-piece suit.

The hair color and wig were recent innovations. My grandfather had always been vain about his appearance and bemoaned his receding hairline. Now his full head of hair gave him a slightly shaggy appearance. Nobody said much about the wig, but the hair dye caused considerable consternation in the family, especially when we were going out in public. My grandfather often left the cheap drugstore dye on too long, turning his eyebrows and mustache a jarring shade of magenta. When he joined us in the library, obviously proud of what he'd done, Gam said, "Oh, for God's sake, Fred."

"Jesus Christ, Dad!" Donald yelled at him.

"For fuck's sake," Rob swore under his breath.

Maryanne, touching his arm, said, "Dad, you can't do that again."

He was standing by his love seat when I came into the library.

"Hello," he said

"Hi, Grandpa. How are you?"

He looked at me and reached for his wallet, so thick with bills I was constantly surprised that it fit in his pocket. He carried a wallet-sized photograph of a half-naked woman in his billfold, and for a second I was worried that he planned to show it to me, as he had when I was twelve.

"Look at this," he had said, sliding the picture out of its slot. A heavily made-up woman, who couldn't have been more than eighteen and might have been younger, smiled innocently at the camera, her hands holding up her naked breasts. Donald had been looking over my grandfather's shoulder. I hadn't known what to say and had looked at him for some indication of how I should respond, but he'd merely leered at the picture.

"What do you think about that?" My grandfather had chuckled. I never heard him laugh. I don't think he ever did. He usually expressed amusement by saying "Ha!" and then sneering.

Now, instead of a picture, my grandfather pulled out a hundred-dollar bill and asked, "Can I buy your hair?"

That was something he'd ask me every time I saw him when I was growing up. I laughed. "Sorry, Grandpa. I need to hang on to it."

Elizabeth walked over carrying a small box in one hand. She looped an arm around my grandfather's elbow and leaned against him. He looked ahead blankly, disengaged his arm, and left the room.

Shortly after, Donald came in with his kids and Rob's stepson. With the exception of Eric, they were all teenagers, the boys tall and chubby and wearing suits. Donald went to sit on the chair by the TV, and Ivanka climbed on his lap. The boys started wrestling. Donald watched the action from his chair, kissing Ivanka or pinching her cheek. Every once in a while, he'd stick his foot out and kick whichever boy was being pinned to the floor. When they had been younger, Donald had wrestled with them—a fight that had basically consisted of his picking them up, throwing them on the ground, and kneeling on them until they cried uncle. As soon as they had gotten big enough to fight back in earnest, he had opted out.

When Liz and I were as far out of harm's way as we could get, she held the box out to me and said, "This is yours."

We didn't exchange gifts outside of Christmas, but I took the box from her, curious, and opened it to find a vintage stainless-steel Timex with a small, plain face and an olive green band.

"Somebody gave it to you for Christmas," she said. "You were only ten, and I thought you were too young to have something that nice. So I took it." She left the room to look for her father.

Later Donald and Rob huddled together in the breakfast room, their shoulders close and their heads down. My grandfather stood nearby, leaning forward almost on the tips of his toes, trying to hear what they were saying.

Fred said, "Donald, Donald." When he didn't respond, my grandfather tugged on Donald's sleeve.

"What, Dad?" he asked without turning around.

"Look at this," Fred said. He held up a page that had been torn out of a magazine, an ad for a limo similar to the one he already owned.

"What about it?"

"Can I get this?"

Donald took the page and handed it to Rob, who folded it in half and slid it onto the table.

"Sure, Pop," Rob said. Donald left the room. Whatever had once tied them together, Fred's remaining sons had given up all pretense of caring what their father thought or wanted. Having served his father's purpose, Donald now treated him with contempt, as if his mental decline were somehow his own fault. Fred had treated his oldest son and his alcoholism the same way, so Donald's attitude wasn't surprising. It was jarring, though, to witness the open contempt. As far as I knew at the time, Donald not only had been my grandfather's favorite, he had also seemed to be the only child of his that he liked. I knew my grandfather could be cruel, but I thought the largest measure of that cruelty was reserved for my father, who, to my shame, I thought had probably deserved it. I didn't know how lonely and frightening life in the House had been at the time of my grandmother's illness all those years ago. I didn't know that my grandfather hadn't taken care of any of his children during the year of Gam's absence or that Donald had been particularly vulnerable to that neglect. And far from supporting and nurturing my father as he ventured out into the world with the sincere intent to be a success, Fred was really only enabling Donald, waiting until he was old enough to be of use.

In 1994, I moved from my Upper East Side apartment to Garden City, a town on Long Island only a fifteen-minute drive from the House. I would take Gam to see her great-grandchildren, my brother's daughter and son, driving her in the red Rolls-Royce my grandfather had bought for her birthday a few years earlier. Behind the large, loose walnut steering wheel, I felt so high up that I could practically see the curvature of the earth. Sometimes Gam and I chatted easily during the forty-five-minute drive, but more often she was moody and taciturn. On days like that, the trip felt interminable. She sometimes smelled strongly of vanilla even when she hadn't been baking. Other times, I would see her out of the corner of my eye surreptitiously slide her hand into her purse and put something into her mouth.

Usually we sat in the library chatting. I was often there when Maryanne made her daily phone call to check in. After answering, Gam covered the receiver and said to me, "It's Maryanne," then, to her daughter, "Guess who's here? Mary." She paused, I guess to give Maryanne a chance to say something such as "Tell her I say hi," but she never did.

Sometimes we went to eat at a local restaurant. One of Gam's favorite places to have lunch was the Sly Fox Inn, a low-key pub directly across the street from the grocery store parking lot where she'd been mugged. We never talked about Dad much, but one day she seemed particularly nostalgic. She reminisced about the trouble he and Billy Drake used to get into, how easily Dad had made her laugh. She went quiet after the waiter came to take our plates. When he asked if we wanted the check Gam didn't answer, so I nodded.

"Mary, he was so sick."

"I know, Gam," I said, assuming she meant his drinking.

"I didn't know what to do."

I thought she was going to cry and said, uselessly, "Gam, it's okay."

"Those last few weeks"—she took a deep breath—"he couldn't get out of bed."

"The day I came by—" I started to ask.

The waiter brought the check.

"Didn't he go to the doctor?" I asked. "I mean, if he was that sick."

"He felt so bad when he heard you'd come to see him."

I waited for her to say something else, but Gam opened her purse. She always paid for lunch. I drove her home in silence.

In 1987, I had spent my junior year abroad in Germany, a place for which I had no affinity, but I'd thought it might please my grandfather since it was the country of his parents' birth. (It didn't.) I had planned to come home for Christmas, and I called my grandparents to ask if I could stay with them.

I'd stood at the pay phone in the hallway of my dorm with a handful of five-mark coins and called the House. "Hi, Grandpa. It's Mary," I'd said when he answered.

"Yes," he had replied.

I explained why I was calling.

"Why can't you stay with your mother?" he had asked.

"I'm allergic to the cats, and I'm afraid I might have an asthma attack."

"Then tell her to get rid of the cats."

It was so much easier being the "nice lady" now.

I saw firsthand how difficult living with my grandfather had become for Gam. My grandfather's odd behavior had started with small things, such as hiding her checkbook. When she confronted him, he accused her of trying to bankrupt him. When she tried to reason with him, he became enraged, leaving her feeling shaken and unsafe. He worried constantly about money, terrified that his fortune was disappearing. My grandfather had never been poor a day in his life, but poverty became his sole preoccupation; he was tortured by the prospect of it.

My grandfather's moods eventually evened out, and the problem for

Gam became the repetition. After getting home from the office in the evening, he'd go upstairs to change, often coming back downstairs wearing a fresh dress shirt and tie but no pants, just his boxers, socks, and dress shoes. "So how is everybody? Okay? Okay. Good night, Toots," he'd say, and head back upstairs, only to descend again a few minutes later.

One evening as Gam and I sat together in the library, my grandfather came in and asked, "Hey, Toots, what's for dinner?"

After she answered, he walked out. A few moments later, he returned. "What's for dinner?" She answered again. He left and returned ten, twelve, fifteen times. With decreasing amounts of patience, she told him "Roast beef and potatoes" every time.

Eventually she lashed out at him. "For God's sake, Fred, stop it! I've already told you."

"Okay, okay, Toots," he said with a nervous laugh, hands raised against her as he bounced up on his toes. "Well, that's that," he said, tucking his thumbs under his suspenders, as though we had just finished a conversation. The gestures were the same as they'd always been, but the glint in his eyes had become dully benign.

He left the room, only to wander in a few minutes later to ask, "What's for dinner?"

Gam pulled me onto the porch—an uninviting square of cement on the side of the House just off the library that decades earlier had been used for family barbecues. It had been so long neglected that I often forgot it existed.

"I swear, Mary," she told me, "he's going to drive me mad." The chairs that had been left out there and long forgotten were so littered with twigs and dead leaves that we remained standing.

"You need to get help," I said. "You should talk to someone."

"I can't leave him." She was close to tears.

"I would have liked to go home again," she once told me wistfully. I didn't understand why she couldn't go back to Scotland, but she adamantly refused to do anything that might look selfish.

On weekends, if they weren't at Mar-a-Lago, my grandparents

would drive to one of their other children's country homes: Robert's in Millbrook, New York; Elizabeth's in Southampton; or Maryanne's in Sparta, New Jersey. They would plan to spend the night, and my grandmother would look forward to a quiet, relaxing weekend with other people. As soon as they arrived at their destination, my grandfather would ask if they could go home. He wouldn't relent until Gam gave up and they got back into the car. The idea of a weekend (or day) retreat had been for Gam's benefit, a chance for her to get out of the House and have company. Eventually the visits became just another form of torture. Like so much else in the family that didn't make sense, they continued doing it anyway.

Gam was in the hospital again. I don't remember what she'd broken, but after the hospital stay, she had the option of going to a rehab facility or having a physical therapist sent to her home. She opted for the rehab facility. "Anything to avoid going back to the House," she told me.

It was better that way. After the mugging, she had had to sleep in a hospital bed in the library for weeks. My grandfather, who'd recovered very well from his hip surgery, hadn't had much to say in the way of commiseration or comfort.

"Everything's great. Right, Toots?" he'd say.

In 1998, we celebrated Father's Day at Donald's apartment at Trump Tower for the first time. It had become too difficult for my grandfather to be in public, so our traditional trip to Peter Luger in Brooklyn was out of the question. It was a family custom to go there twice a year, on Father's Day and my grandfather's birthday.

Peter Luger was a deeply strange, very expensive restaurant that charged extra for bad service and accepted only cash, check, or a Peter Luger charge card (which my grandfather possessed). The menu was limited, and whether you asked for them or not, huge platters of sliced beefsteak tomatoes and white onions arrived, accompanied by tiny ceramic dishes of hash fries and creamed spinach that usually went untouched. A side of beef was brought out on trays, punctuated with little plastic cows in varying shades ranging from red (still mooing) and pink (almost able to crawl across the table) to—actually, I don't know. All of our little cows were red and pink. Most of us ordered Cokes, which were served in six-ounce bottles; because of the legendarily bad service, that meant at the end of the evening the table was littered with the wreckage of a couple of cow carcasses, dozens of Coke bottles, and plates full of food nobody in my family ever ate.

The meal wasn't over until my grandfather had sucked the marrow out of the bones, which, given his mustache, was a sight to behold.

Since I'd stopped eating meat in college, dinner at Peter Luger had become a challenge. I'd once made the mistake of ordering salmon, which took up half the table and tasted about as good as you might expect salmon from a steak house would taste. Eventually my meal consisted of Coke, the little potatoes, and an iceberg wedge salad.

I wouldn't miss the rude waiters, but I hoped there would at least be something for me to eat at Donald's.

I made the mistake of arriving at the penthouse early and alone. Although Donald and Marla were still married, she was already a distant memory, replaced by his new girlfriend, Melania, a twenty-eight-year-old Slovenian model whom I'd never met. They sat on an uncomfortable-looking love seat in the foyer, a large, undefined space. Everything was marble, gold leaf, mirrored walls, white walls, and frescoes. I'm not sure how he managed it, but Donald's apartment felt even colder and less like a home than the House did.

Melania was five years younger than I was. She sat slightly sideways next to Donald with her ankles crossed. I was struck by how smooth she looked. After Robert and Blaine had met her for the first time, Rob told me that Melania had barely spoken throughout the entire meal.

"Maybe her English isn't very good," I said.

"No," he scoffed. "She knows what she's there for." Clearly it wasn't for her sparkling conversation.

As soon as I sat down, Donald started telling Melania about the time he'd hired me to write *The Art of the Comeback* and then launched into his version of my "back from the brink" redemption story. He thought it was something we had in common: we'd both hit rock bottom and then somehow clawed our way back to the top (in his case) or just back (in mine).

"You dropped out of college, right?"

"Yes, Donald, I did." It was exactly how I wanted to be introduced to someone I'd never met. I was also surprised he even knew about it

"It was really bad for a while—and then she started doing drugs."

"Whoa," I said, holding up my hands.

"Really?" said Melania, suddenly interested.

"No, no, no. I've never done drugs in my life."

He slid me a look and smiled. He was embellishing the story for effect, and he knew I knew it. "She was a total disaster," he said, smiling more broadly.

Donald loved comeback stories, and he understood that the deeper the hole you crawled out of, the better billing your triumphant comeback would get. Which was exactly how he experienced his own journey. By conflating my dropping out of college and his hiring me to write his book (while throwing in a fictional drug addiction), he concocted a better story that somehow had him playing the role of my savior. Of course, between my dropping out of school and his hiring me, I'd dropped back into school, graduated, and gotten a master's degree—all without taking any drugs at all. There was no point in setting the record straight, however; there never was with him. The story was for his benefit as much as anybody else's, and by the time the doorbell rang, he probably already believed his version of events. When the three of us rose to greet the new guests, I realized that Melania had said only one word during our time together.

On June 11, 1999, Fritz called to tell me our grandfather had been taken to Long Island Jewish Medical Center, another Queens hospital my grandparents had patronized in recent years. He said it was likely the end.

I drove the ten minutes from my house and found that the room was already full. Gam sat in the only chair near the bed; Elizabeth stood next to her, holding my grandfather's hand.

After saying hello, I stood by the window next to Robert's wife, Blaine. She said, "We're supposed to be in London with Prince Charles." I realized she was talking to me—something she rarely did.

"Oh," I said.

"He invited us to one of his polo matches. I can't believe we had to cancel." She sounded exasperated and made no effort to lower her voice.

I could have topped that story. In a week I was supposed to be getting married on a beach in Maui. Nobody in the family knew; they'd always been spectacularly uninterested in my personal life (when necessary, I asked a guy friend to accompany me to any family occasion that required a plus one) and never asked about my boyfriends or relationships.

A couple of years earlier, Gam and I had been talking about Princess Diana's funeral, and when she had said with some vehemence, "It's a disgrace they're letting that little faggot Elton John sing at the service," I'd realized it was better that she didn't know I was living with and engaged to a woman.

Seeing how serious my grandfather's condition was, I had a terrible feeling that when I got home, I'd have to break the news to my fiancée that, after months of planning and overcoming several logistical nightmares, our mostly secret wedding would have to be postponed.

I noticed a hush in the room, as if everybody had run out of small talk at the same time. We were reduced for the moment to listening to my grandfather's uneven breathing: a ragged, uncertain inhalation, followed by an unnatural pause for longer than seemed safe until finally he exhaled.

CHAPTER ELEVEN

The Only Currency

Fred Trump died on June 25, 1999. The following day, his obituary was published in the *New York Times* under the banner "Fred C. Trump, Postwar Master Builder of Housing for Middle Class, Dies at 93." The obituary writer made a point of contrasting Fred's status as "a self-made man" with "his flamboyant son Donald." My grandfather's propensity for picking up unused nails at his construction sites to hand back to his carpenters the next day was noted before the details of his birth. The *Times* also repeated the family line that Donald had built his own business with minimal help from my grandfather—"a small amount of money"—a statement that the paper itself would refute twenty years later.

We sat in the library, each with our own copy of the *Times*. Robert was raked over the coals by his siblings for having told the *Times* that my grandfather's estate was worth between $250 million and $300 million. "Never, never give them numbers," Maryanne lectured him, as if he were a stupid kid. He stood there shamefaced, cracking his knuckles and bouncing on the balls of his feet, just as my grandfather used to do, as if suddenly imagining the ensuing tax bill. The valuation was absurdly low—eventually we would learn that the empire was probably worth four times that—but Maryanne and Donald would never have admitted that it was even that much.

Later we stood upstairs in the Madison Room at the Frank E. Campbell Funeral Chapel on Manhattan's Upper East Side, the most exclusive and expensive bereavement services provider in the city, smiling and shaking hands as a seemingly endless line of visitors passed through.

Overall, more than eight hundred people moved through the rooms. Some were there to pay their respects, including rival real estate developers such as Sam LeFrak, New York governor George Pataki, former Senator Al D'Amato, and comedian and future *Celebrity Apprentice* contestant Joan Rivers. The rest were most likely there to catch a glimpse of Donald.

On the day of the funeral, Marble Collegiate Church was filled to capacity. During the service, from beginning to end, everyone had a role to play. It was all extremely well choreographed. Elizabeth read my grandfather's "favorite poem," and the rest of the siblings gave eulogies, as did my brother, who spoke on behalf of my dad, and my cousin David, who represented the grandchildren. Mostly they told stories about my grandfather, although my brother was the only one who came close to humanizing him. For the most part, in ways both oblique and direct, the emphasis was on my grandfather's material success, his "killer" instinct, and his talent for saving a buck. Donald was the only one to deviate from the script. In a cringe-inducing turn, his eulogy devolved into a paean to his own greatness. It was so embarrassing that Maryanne later told her son not to allow any of her siblings to speak at her funeral.

Rudolph Giuliani, New York City's mayor at the time, also spoke.

When the service was over, the six oldest grandchildren (Tiffany was too young) accompanied the casket to the hearse as honorary pallbearers, which meant, as was often the case in our family, that others did the heavy lifting while we got the credit.

All of the streets from Fifth Avenue and 45th Street to the Midtown Tunnel more than sixteen blocks away had been closed to cars and pedestrians, so our motorcade, with a police escort, slid easily out of the city. It was a quick trip to All Faiths Cemetery in Middle Village, Queens, for the burial.

We drove back to the city just as quickly, but with less fanfare, for lunch at Donald's apartment. Afterward, I accompanied my grand-mother back to the House. The two of us sat in the library and chatted for a while. She seemed tired but relieved. It had been a very long day; a very long few years, actually. Other than the live-in maid, who was asleep upstairs, it was just the two of us. I was supposed to be on my honeymoon. I stayed with her until she was ready to go to bed.

When she said she was ready for bed, I asked her if she wanted me to stay or if there was anything I could get for her before I left.

"No, dear, I'm fine."

I bent over to kiss her cheek. She smelled like vanilla. "You are my favorite person," I told her. It wasn't true, but I said it because I loved her. I said it, too, because nobody else had bothered to stay with her after her husband of sixty-three years had been put in the ground.

"Good," she replied. "I should be."

And then I left her alone in that large, quiet, empty house.

Two weeks after my grandfather's funeral, I was home when a DHL truck pulled up and delivered a yellow envelope containing a copy of my grandfather's will. I read through it twice to be sure I hadn't mis-understood anything. I had promised my brother I'd call him as soon as I knew anything, but I was reluctant to do so. Fritz and Lisa's third child, William, had been born hours after my grandfather's funeral. Twenty-four hours after that, he'd begun having seizures. He had been in the neonatal intensive care unit ever since. They had two young chil-dren at home, and Fritz had to work. I had no idea how they were man-aging all of it.

I hated to be the bearer of more bad news, but he needed to know.

I called him.

"So what's the deal?" he asked.

"Nothing," I told him. "We got nothing,"

A few days later, I got a call from Rob. As far as I could remember, he had only ever called me before to let me know when Gam was in the hospital. He acted as if everything were fine. If I signed off on the will, he implied, everything would be great. And he did need my signature in order for the will to be released for probate. Though it's true that my grandfather disinherited me and my brother—that is, instead of splitting what would have been my father's 20 percent share of his estate between me and my brother, he had divided it evenly among his four other children—we were included in a bequest made separately to all of the grandchildren, an amount that proved to be less than a tenth of 1 percent of what my aunts and uncles had inherited. In the context of the entire estate it was a very small amount of money, and it must have infuriated Robert that it gave me and Fritz the power to hold up the distribution of the assets.

Days passed, and I couldn't bring myself to sign. In the breadth and concision of its cruelty, the will was a stunning document that very much resembled my parents' divorce agreement.

For a while, Robert called me every day. Maryanne and Donald had assigned him to be the point person; Donald didn't want to be bothered, and Maryanne's husband, John, had been diagnosed with esophageal cancer, and his prognosis was not good.

"Cash in your chips, Honeybunch," Rob said repeatedly, as if that would make me forget what was in the will. No matter how many times he said it, though, my brother and I had agreed not to sign anything until we had some idea of what our options were.

Eventually Rob began to lose patience. Fritz and I were holding everything up; the will couldn't go to probate until all of the beneficiaries had signed off. When I told Rob that Fritz and I weren't yet willing to take that step, he suggested we get together to discuss it.

At our first meeting, when we asked Rob to explain why my grandfather had done what he had, Rob said, "Listen, your grandfather didn't give a shit about you. And not just you, he didn't give a shit about any of his grandchildren."

"We're being treated worse because our father died," I said.

"No, not at all."

When we pointed out that our cousins would still benefit from what their parents were getting from my grandfather, Rob said, "Any of them could be disowned at any time. Donny was going to join the army or some bullshit like that, and Donald and Ivana told him if he did, they'd disown him in a second."

"Our father didn't have that luxury," I said.

Rob sat back. I could see him trying to recalibrate. "It's pretty simple," he said. "As far as your grandfather was concerned, dead is dead. He only cared about his living children."

I wanted to point out that my grandfather hadn't cared about Rob, either, but Fritz intervened. "Rob," he said, "this just isn't fair."

I lost track of how many meetings the three of us had between July and October 1999. There was a brief respite in September while I was in Hawaii for my postponed wedding and honeymoon.

At the very beginning of our discussions, Fritz, Robert, and I agreed that we would leave Gam out of it. I assumed she had no idea how we'd been treated in my grandfather's will and saw no reason to upset her. Hopefully we would be able to resolve everything, and she'd never have to know there had been a problem at all. I spoke to her every day while I was away and, once back in New York, resumed my visits to her. The negotiations, if they could even be called that, also resumed. There was a numbing sameness to our conversations. No matter what Fritz and I said, Rob came back with his clichés and canned responses. We remained at a standstill.

I asked him about Midland Associates, the management company my grandfather had set up decades earlier in order to avoid paying certain taxes and benefit his children. Midland owned a group of seven buildings (including Sunnyside Towers and the Highlander) that were referred to in my family as "the mini-empire." I knew very little about it—none of my trustees had ever explained what role it played or how money was generated—but I received a check every few months. We wanted to know how or if my grandfather's death would affect the partnership going forward.

We weren't asking for a specific dollar amount or a percentage of the estate, just some assurance that the assets we already had would be secure in the future and if, given the family's enormous wealth, there was anything they could see their way clear to doing as far as my grandfather's estate was concerned. As the executors and, along with Elizabeth, sole beneficiaries, Maryanne, Donald, and Robert had a wide latitude in that area, but Rob remained noncommittal.

At our final meeting, in the bar of the Drake Hotel on 56th Street and Park Avenue, it was clear that Robert had begun to understand that we weren't going to back down. Prior to that, despite the unpleasant things he'd been saying to us, he had maintained an affable "Hey, kids, I'm just the messenger" attitude. That day he reminded us, once again, that my grandfather had hated our mother and had been afraid his money would fall into her hands.

That was laughable, because for more than twenty-five years my mother had lived according to the terms the Trumps had set, following their directions to the letter. She had lived in the same poorly maintained apartment in Jamaica, Queens; her alimony and child support payments had rarely been increased, yet she had never asked for more.

Finally, Fred had disowned us because he could. The people who'd been assigned to protect us, at least financially, were our trustees—Maryanne, Donald, Robert, and Irwin Durben—but they apparently had little interest in protecting us, especially at their own expense.

Rob leaned forward, suddenly serious. "Listen, if you *don't* sign this will, if you think of suing us, we will bankrupt Midland Associates and you will be paying taxes on money you don't have for the rest of your lives."

There was nothing left to say after that. Either Fritz and I gave in, or we fought. Neither option was a good one.

We consulted with Irwin, who felt like the only ally we had left. He was incensed about how poorly our grandfather had treated us in the will. When we told him how Robert had responded when asked about

Midland Associates and our share in other Trump entities, he said, "Your share of the ground leases under Shore Haven and Beach Haven alone are priceless. If they're not going to do anything for you, you're going to have to sue them."

I had no idea what a ground lease was, let alone that I had a share in two of them, but I knew what priceless meant. And I trusted Irwin. Based on his recommendation, Fritz and I made a decision.

After all those months, William was still in the hospital, and Fritz and Lisa were feeling overwhelmed. I told him I'd take care of it and called Rob that afternoon.

"Is there anything you guys can do, Rob?" I asked.

"Sign the will, and we'll see."

"Really?"

"Your father's dead," he said.

"I *know* he's dead, Rob. But *we're* not." I was so sick of having that conversation.

He paused. "Maryanne, Donald, and I are simply following Dad's wishes. Your grandfather didn't want you or Fritz, or especially your mother, to get anything."

I took a deep breath. "This is going nowhere," I said. "Fritz and I are going to hire an attorney."

As if a switch had been flipped, Robert screamed, "You do whatever the fuck you need to do!" and slammed the phone down.

The next day, there was a message from Gam on my answering machine when I got home. "Mary, it's your grandmother," she said tersely. She never referred to herself that way. It was always "Gam."

I called her back right away.

"Your uncle Robert tells me you and your brother are suing for twenty percent of your grandfather's estate."

I felt blindsided and said nothing right away. Obviously Rob had broken our agreement and told my grandmother his version of what we'd been discussing. But the other thing that held me up was that my grandmother spoke as if our getting what would have been my father's share of the estate was somehow wrong and unseemly. I was confused—about loyalty, about love, about the limits of both. I'd thought I was part of the family. I'd gotten it all wrong.

"Gam, we haven't asked for anything. I don't know what Rob told you, but we're not suing anybody."

"You'd better not be." ·

"We're just trying to figure this out, that's all."

"Do you know what your father was worth when he died?" she said. "A whole lot of nothing."

There was a pause and then a click. She'd hung up on me.

CHAPTER TWELVE

The Debacle

I sat there with the phone in my hand, not knowing what to do next. It was one of those moments that changes everything—both what came before and what will come after—and it was too big to process.

I called my brother, and as soon as I heard his voice, I burst into tears.

He called Gam to see if he could explain what we were really asking for, but they had basically the same conversation. Her parting shot to him was slightly different, though: "When your father died, he didn't have two nickels to rub together." In the world of my family, that was the only thing that mattered. If your only currency is money, that's the only lens through which you determine worth; somebody who has accomplished in that context as little as my father was worth nothing—even if he happened to be your son. Further, if my father died penniless, his children weren't entitled to anything.

My grandfather had every right to change his will as he saw fit. My aunts and uncles had every right to follow his instructions to the letter, despite the fact that none of them deserved their share of Fred's fortune any more than my father did. If not for an accident of birth, none of them would have been a multimillionaire. Prosecutors and federal judges don't typically have $20 million cottages in Palm Beach. Executive assistants don't have weekend homes in Southampton. (Although, to be fair, Maryanne and Elizabeth were the only two of the siblings, other than my father, to work outside of the family business.)

Still, they acted as if they had earned every penny of my grandfather's wealth and that money was so tied up in their sense of self-worth that letting any of it go was not an option.

On Irwin's advice we approached Jack Barnosky, a partner at Farrell Fritz, the largest law firm in Nassau County. Jack, a pompous, self-satisfied man, agreed to take us on as clients. His strategy was to prove that my grandfather's 1990 will should be overturned: Fred Trump had not been of sound mind at the time the will was signed, and he had been under the undue influence of his children.

Less than a week after we served the executors, Jack received a letter from Lou Laurino, a short, wiry pit bull of a lawyer who was representing my grandfather's estate. The medical insurance that had been provided to us by Trump Management since we were born had been revoked. Everyone in the Trump family was covered by it. My brother depended upon this insurance to pay for my nephew's crushing medical expenses. When William had first fallen ill, Robert had promised Fritz that they would take care of everything; he should just send the bills to the office.

Taking away our insurance didn't benefit them at all; it was merely a way to cause us more pain and make us more desperate. William was out of the hospital by then, but he was still susceptible to seizures, which more than once had put him in a state of cardiac arrest so severe that he would not have survived without CPR. He still required round-the-clock nursing care.

The family all knew this, but none of them objected, not even my grandmother, who was as aware as anybody that her own desperately ill great-grandchild would probably need expensive medical care for the rest of his life.

Fritz and I had no choice but to launch another lawsuit to make them reinstate William's medical insurance. The suit required depositions and affidavits from the doctors and nurses responsible for William's care. It was time consuming and stressful and culminated in an appearance in front of a judge.

Laurino defended the cancellation of the insurance by first claiming that we had no right to expect the insurance in perpetuity. It was, rather, a gift that had been bestowed upon us out of the goodness of my grandfather's heart. He also downplayed William's condition, insisting that the round-the-clock nurses who attended to William and had saved his life more than once were overpriced babysitters. If Fritz and Lisa were worried that their infant son might have another seizure, he said, they should just learn CPR.

The depositions did nothing to help us. I couldn't believe what a terrible interlocutor Jack was. He failed to follow up and went off on tangents. Despite the fact that Fritz and I had prepared long lists of questions for him, he rarely, if ever, referred to them. Robert, much more detached than the last time I'd spoken to him, reiterated my grandfather's hatred of my mother as his central justification for the disinheritance; Maryanne angrily referred to me and my brother as "absentee grandchildren." I thought of all the times she had called the House when I was visiting my grandmother; now I understood why she'd never told my grandmother to say hi. My grandfather, she said, had been furious with us because we had never spent time with our grandmother, completely ignoring the history of the last decade. Apparently, my grandfather had also hated that Fritz never wore a tie and I, as a teenager, had dressed in baggy sweaters and jeans. When he was deposed, Donald didn't know or couldn't remember anything, a kind of strategic forgetfulness he has employed many times to evade blame or scrutiny. All three of them claimed in their sworn depositions that my grandfather had been "sharp as a tack" until just before he died.

During that time, my aunt Elizabeth ran into a family friend, who later relayed the exchange to my brother. "Can you believe what Fritz and Mary are doing?" she asked him. "All they care about is the money." Of course wills are about money, but in a family that has only one currency, wills are also about love. I thought Liz might have understood that. She had no power. Her opinion about the situation wouldn't have mattered to anybody but me and my brother, but it still hurt that she was toeing the party line. Even a silent, powerless ally would have been better than none at all.

After almost two years, with legal bills piling up and having made no progress on any kind of settlement, we had to decide whether to take our family to court. William's condition remained serious, and a trial would have taken the kind of energy and focus my brother didn't have. Reluctantly, we decided to settle.

Maryanne, Donald, and Robert refused to settle unless we agreed to let them buy our shares of the assets we'd inherited from our father—his 20 percent of the mini-empire and the "priceless" ground leases.

My aunts and uncles submitted a property valuation to Jack Barnosky, and, using their figures, he and Lou Laurino arrived at a settlement figure that was likely based on suspect numbers. Jack told us that, short of a trial, it was the best we could expect. "We know they're lying," he said, "but it's 'He said, she said.' Besides, your grandfather's estate is only worth around thirty million dollars." That was only a tenth of the estimate Robert had given the *New York Times* in 1999, which itself would turn out to be only 25 percent of the estate's actual value.

Fred no doubt believed that my dad had been given the same tools, the same advantages, and the same opportunities as Donald had. If Freddy had thrown them all away, that wasn't his father's fault. If, despite them, my dad had continued to be a terrible provider, my brother and I should consider ourselves lucky that there were trust funds our father couldn't squander when he was alive. Whatever happened to us after that had nothing to do with Fred Trump. He had done his part; we had no right to expect more.

While the lawsuits were still in progress, I received word that, after a brief illness, Gam had died on August 7, 2000, at Long Island Jewish Medical Center, just as my grandfather had. She was eighty-eight.

If I had known she was sick, I think I would have tried to see her, but the fact that she hadn't asked to see me clarified just how easy it had been for us to let each other go. We had never spoken after that last phone conversation, just as I had not spoken again to Robert, Donald, Maryanne, or Elizabeth. It had never occurred to me to try.

Fritz and I decided to attend Gam's funeral, but, knowing we were unwelcome, we stood in one of the overflow rooms at the back of Marble Collegiate Church. Along with a couple of Donald's security guards, we watched the service on a closed-circuit monitor.

The eulogies were remarkable only for what was not said. There was a lot of speculation about my grandparents' reunion in Heaven, but my father, their oldest son, who had been dead for almost twenty-seven years, was not mentioned at all. He didn't even appear in my grandmother's obituary.

I received a copy of Gam's will a few weeks after she died. It was a carbon copy of my grandfather's, with one exception: my brother and I had been removed from the section outlining the bequests for her grandchildren. My father and his entire line had now been effectively erased.

PART FOUR

The Worst Investment Ever Made

CHAPTER THIRTEEN

The Political Is Personal

Nearly a decade would pass before I saw my family again, in October 2009 at my cousin Ivanka's wedding to Jared Kushner. I had no idea why I'd received the invitation—which was printed on the same heavy-gauge stationery favored by the Trump Organization.

As the limo I'd taken from my home on Long Island approached the clubhouse at Donald's golf club in Bedminster, New Jersey, which looked eerily like the House, I was unsure what to expect. Ushers handed out black shawls, which made me feel a little less exposed as I wrapped one around my shoulders.

The outdoor ceremony took place beneath a large white tent. Gilt chairs were lined up in rows on either side of a gilt-trimmed runway carpet. The traditional Jewish chuppah, covered in white roses, was about the size of my house. Donald stood awkwardly in a yarmulke. Before the vows, Jared's father, Charles, who'd been released from prison three years earlier, rose to tell us that when Jared had first introduced him to Ivanka, he had thought she would never be good enough to join his family. It was only after she had committed to converting to Judaism and worked hard to make it happen that he had begun to think she might be worthy of them after all. Considering that Charles had been convicted of hiring a prostitute to seduce his brother-in-law, taping their illicit encounter, and then sending the recording to his sister at his nephew's engagement party, I found his condescension a bit out of line. After the ceremony, my brother, my sister-in-law, and I entered the clubhouse.

As I walked down the hallway, I saw my uncle Rob. My last exchange with him had been when he'd hung up on me in 1999 after I had told him that Fritz and I were hiring a lawyer to contest my grandfather's will. As I approached him now, he surprised me by breaking into a smile. He put his hand out, then leaned down—he was much taller than I was even in my heels—shook my hand, and kissed me on the cheek, the typical Trump greeting.

"Honeybunch! How are you?" he said brightly. Before I could answer, he said, "You know, I've been thinking that the statute of limitations on family estrangement has passed." Then, bouncing on the balls of his feet, he smacked a closed fist into his open palm in a not-quite-accurate imitation of my grandfather.

"That sounds good to me," I said. We spent a couple of minutes exchanging pleasantries. When we were done, I walked up the stairs to the cocktail reception, where I spotted Donald speaking to somebody I recognized—a mayor or a governor—although I can't recall who it was.

"Hi, Donald," I said, as I walked toward them.

"Mary! You look great." He shook my hand and kissed my cheek, as Rob had. "It's good to see you."

"It's good to see you, too." It was a relief to discover that things between us were pleasant and civil. Having established that, I gave way to the next person in the lengthening line of people, some of them waiting to congratulate the father of the bride. But *The Apprentice* had just concluded its eighth season, so it's just as likely that many of them were simply there for the photo op. "Have fun," he called after me as I walked away.

The reception was being held in an enormous ballroom quite a distance from the hors d'oeuvres. Along the way I saw my aunt Liz in the distance, chasing after her husband. I caught her eye and waved. She waved back and said, "Hi, sweetie pie." But she didn't stop, and that was the last I saw of her. I walked past voluminous bunting and the highly polished dance floor and finally found my place at the second cousins' table on the periphery of the ballroom. In the distance I could hear the occasional *thwap* of rotors as helicopters landed and took off.

After the first course had been served, I decided to find Maryanne. As I wound my way through the tables, Donald took to the stage to give his toast. If I hadn't known who he was talking about, I would have thought he was toasting his secretary's daughter.

I spotted Maryanne and paused. Fritz and I would not have been invited to Ivanka's wedding without Maryanne's approval. She didn't see me until I was standing right in front of her.

"Hi, Aunt Maryanne."

It took her a few seconds to realize who I was. "Mary." She didn't smile. "How are you?" she asked, her expression rigid.

"Everything's great. My daughter just turned eight, and—"

"I didn't know you had a daughter."

Of course she didn't know I had a daughter or that I was raising her with the woman I'd married after my grandfather's funeral and then divorced or that I had recently received my doctorate in clinical psychology. But she acted as if her lack of such knowledge was an insult to her. The rest of our brief conversation was equally tense. She mentioned that Ivana had missed Ivanka's wedding shower but said, sotto voce, that she couldn't discuss why.

I retreated to my table, and when I realized the vegetarian meal I'd ordered had not arrived, I ordered a martini in its stead. The olives would suffice.

Sometime later, I saw Maryanne, looking determined, head toward us as if on a mission. She walked straight up to my brother and said, "We need to talk about the elephant in the room." Then, gesturing to include me, "The three of us."

A few weeks after Ivanka and Jared's wedding, Fritz and I met with Maryanne and Robert at her apartment on the Upper East Side. It wasn't clear to me why Rob was there, but I thought perhaps he planned to make good on his claim that the "statute of limitations" on family estrangement had passed. I took it as a good sign, but as the afternoon wore on, I became less sure. We didn't discuss anything that seemed pertinent. As we sat in the living room with its spectacular view of Central Park and the Metropolitan Museum of Art, Maryanne made passing references to "the debacle," as she called the lawsuit, but nobody else seemed eager to go down that road.

Rob leaned forward in his chair, and I hoped finally we were going to start dealing with the so-called elephant in the room. Instead he told a story.

Ten years earlier, Rob had still been working for Donald in Atlantic City when Donald's financial situation was dire. His investors were getting hammered, the banks were after him, and his personal life was in shambles. When things were at their worst, Donald had called Rob with a request.

"Listen, Rob, I don't know how this is all going to end," he had said. "But it's tough, and I might drop dead of a heart attack. If anything happens to me, I want you to make sure Marla will be okay."

"Sure, Donald. Just tell me what you want me to do."

"Get her ten million dollars."

I thought, *Holy shit, that's a lot of money!* at the same moment that Rob said, "What a cheap bastard."

Rob laughed at the memory as I sat there stunned, wondering how much money those people had. Last I'd heard, $10 million would have been one-third of my grandfather's entire estate.

"Around the same time, Donald called to tell me I was one of his three favorite people," Maryanne said. "Apparently he forgot he had three children." (Tiffany and Barron were still to come.)

We never met with Rob again, but Fritz and I, separately and together, had lunch occasionally with Maryanne. For the first time in my life, I got to know my aunt. Not since I'd spent time with Donald while I was writing his book had I felt a little bit as though I were part of the family.

A couple of months after my aunts' April 2017 birthday party, I was in my living room lacing up my sneakers when the front doorbell rang. I don't know why I answered it. I almost never did. Seventy-five percent of the time it was a Jehovah's Witness or Mormon missionaries. The rest of the time, it was somebody wanting me to sign a petition.

When I opened the door, the only thing that registered was that the woman standing there, with her shock of curly blond hair and dark-rimmed glasses, was someone I didn't know. Her khakis, button-down shirt, and messenger bag placed her out of Rockville Centre.

"Hi. My name is Susanne Craig. I'm a reporter for the *New York Times*."

Journalists had stopped contacting me a long time before. With the exception of David Corn from *Mother Jones* and somebody from *Frontline*, the only other person to leave a message before the election had been from *Inside Edition*. Nothing I had to say about my uncle would have mattered before November 2016; why would anybody want to hear from me now?

The futility of it annoyed me, so I said, "It is so not cool that you're showing up at my house."

"I understand. I'm sorry. But we're working on a very important story about your family's finances, and we think you could really help us."

"I can't talk to you."

"At least take my card. If you change your mind, you can call me anytime."

"I don't talk to reporters," I said. I took her card anyway.

A few weeks later, I fractured the fifth metatarsal of my left foot. For the next four months, I was a prisoner in my home, my foot elevated at all times as I sat on the couch.

I received a letter from Susanne Craig reiterating her belief that I had documents that could help "rewrite the history of the President of the United States," as she put it. I ignored the letter. But she persisted.

After a month of sitting on the couch, scrolling through Twitter with the news constantly on in the background, I watched in real time as Donald shredded norms, endangered alliances, and trod upon the vulnerable. The only thing about it that surprised me was the increasing number of people willing to enable him.

As I watched our democracy disintegrating and people's lives unraveling because of my uncle's policies, I kept thinking about Susanne Craig's letter. I found her business card and called her. I told her that I wanted to help but I no longer had any documents relating to our lawsuit years before.

"Jack Barnosky might still have them," she said.

Ten days later I was on my way to his office.

The headquarters of Farrell Fritz was located in one of two oblong buildings sheathed in blue glass. Bitterly cold air pushed between them across the wide-open space of the enormous parking lot. It's impossible to park anywhere near the entrance, so after I found a spot, it took me ten minutes to get to the lobby on my crutches. I negotiated the escalator and the marble floors very carefully.

By the time I arrived at my destination, I was tired and overheated. Thirty banker's boxes lined two walls and filled a bookshelf. The room's only other contents were a desk and a chair. Jack's secretary had kindly put out a pad of paper, a pen, and some paper clips. I dropped my bags, leaned my crutches against the wall, and half fell into the desk chair. None of the boxes was labeled; I had no idea where to start.

It took me about an hour to familiarize myself with the contents of the boxes and compile a list, which required wheeling around the room on my chair and lifting boxes onto the desk while standing on one leg. When Jack stopped by, I was flushed and soaking wet. He reminded me that I couldn't take any documents out of the room. "They belong to your brother, too, and I need his permission," which wasn't at all true.

When he turned to leave, I called after him, "Jack, wait a second. Can you remind me why we decided to settle the lawsuit?"

"Well, you were getting concerned about the costs, and, as you know, we don't take cases on contingency. Although we knew they were lying to us, it was 'He said, she said.' Besides, your grandfather's estate was only worth thirty million dollars." It was almost word for word what he'd told me when I had last seen him almost twenty years earlier.

"Ah, okay. Thanks." I was holding in my hands documents that proved the estate had actually been worth close to a billion dollars when he died; I just didn't know it yet.

After I was sure he had gone, I grabbed copies of my grandfather's wills, floppy disks with all of the depositions from the lawsuit, and some of my grandfather's bank records—all of which I was legally entitled to as part of the lawsuit—and stuffed them into my bags.

Sue came by my house the next day to pick up the documents and drop off a burner phone so we could communicate more securely going forward. We weren't taking any chances.

On my third trip to Farrell Fritz, I methodically went through every box and discovered that there were two copies of *everything*. I mentioned the fact to Jack's secretary and suggested that it obviated the need to get my brother's permission, which was a relief since I didn't want to involve him. I would leave a set of documents for him in the unlikely event he ever wanted one.

I was just beginning to look for the list of material the *Times* wanted when I got a message from Jack: I could take whatever I wanted, as long as I left a copy. I hadn't been prepared for that. In fact, I had plans to meet Sue and her colleagues Russ Buettner and David Barstow (the other two journalists working on the story) at my house at 1:00 with whatever I'd managed to smuggle out. I texted Sue with the news that I'd be late.

At 3:00, I drove to the loading dock beneath the building, and nineteen boxes were loaded into the back of the borrowed truck I was driving since I couldn't work the clutch in my own car.

It was just beginning to get dark when I pulled into my driveway. The three reporters were waiting for me in David's white SUV, which sported a pair of reindeer antlers and a huge red nose wired to the grill. When I showed them the boxes, there were hugs all around. It was the happiest I'd felt in months.

When Sue, Russ, and David left, I was exhausted and relieved. It had been a head-spinning few weeks. I hadn't fully grasped how much of a risk I was taking. If anybody in my family found out what I was doing, there would be repercussions—I knew how vindictive they were—but there was no way to gauge how serious the consequences might be. Anything would pale in comparison to what they'd already done. I finally felt as though I might be able to make a difference after all.

In the past, there had been nothing I could do that would be significant enough, so I hadn't tried very hard. Because being good or doing good didn't count for much; whatever you did had to be extraordinary. You couldn't just be a prosecutor; you had to be the best prosecutor in the country, you had to be a federal judge. You couldn't just fly planes; you had to be a professional pilot for a major carrier at the dawn of the jet age. For a long time, I blamed my grandfather for my feeling this way. But none of us realized that the expectation of being "the best" in my grandfather's view had applied only to my father (who had failed) and Donald (who had wildly exceeded Fred's expectations).

When I finally realized that my grandfather didn't care what I accomplished or contributed and that my own unrealistic expectations were paralyzing me, I still felt that only a grand gesture would set it right. It wasn't enough for me to volunteer at an organization helping Syrian refugees; I had to take Donald down.

After the election, Donald called his big sister, ostensibly to find out how he was doing. Of course, he thought he already knew the answer; otherwise he wouldn't have made the call in the first place. He merely wanted her to confirm very strongly that he was doing a fantastic job.

When she said, "Not that good," Donald immediately went on offense.

"That's nasty," he said. She could see the sneer on his face. Then, seemingly apropos of nothing, he asked her, "Maryanne, where would you be without me?" It was a smug reference to the fact that Maryanne owed her first federal judgeship to Donald because Roy Cohn had done him (and her) a favor all those years ago.

My aunt has always insisted that she'd earned her position on the bench entirely on her own merits, and she shot back at him, "If you say that one more time, I will *level* you."

But it was an empty threat. Although Maryanne had prided herself on being the only person on the planet Donald ever listened to, those days were long past, which was illustrated not long after, in June 2018. On the eve of Donald's first summit with North Korean dictator Kim Jong-un, Maryanne called the White House and left a message with his secretary: "Tell him his older sister called with a little sisterly advice. Prepare. Learn from those who know what they are doing. Stay away from Dennis Rodman. And leave his Twitter at home."

He ignored all of it. The *Politico* headline the following day read "Trump Says Kim Meeting Will Be About 'Attitude,' Not Prep Work." If Maryanne had ever had any sway over her little brother, it was gone now. Aside from the requisite birthday call, they didn't speak much after that.

While they were working on the article, the *Times* reporters invited me to join them for a tour of my grandfather's properties. On the morning of January 10, 2018, they picked me up in David's SUV, still adorned with its antlers and red nose, at the Jamaica train station. We started at the Highlander, where I'd grown up, and over the course of the day we traversed snow drifts and patches of ice in an effort to visit as much of the Trump empire as possible.

After nine hours we still hadn't managed to see all of it. I had traded in my crutches for a cane by then but was still exhausted, mentally and physically, when I got home. I tried to make sense of what I'd seen. I'd always known that my grandfather owned buildings, but I'd had no idea just how many. More disturbing, my father had apparently owned 20 percent of some of the buildings I'd never heard of before.

On October 2, 2018, the New York Times published an almost 14,000-word article, the longest in its history, revealing the long litany of potentially fraudulent and criminal activities my grandfather, aunts, and uncles had engaged in.

Through the extraordinary reporting of the Times team, I learned more about my family's finances than I'd ever known.

Donald's lawyer, Charles J. Harder, predictably denied the allegations, saying: "The New York Times's allegations of fraud and tax evasion are 100 percent false, and highly defamatory. There was no fraud or tax evasion by anyone." But the investigative reporters laid out a devastating case. Over the course of Fred's life, he and my grandmother had transferred hundreds of millions of dollars to their children. While my grandfather was alive, Donald alone had received the equivalent of $413 million, much of it through questionable means: loans that he had never repaid, investments in properties that had never matured; essentially gifts that had never been taxed. That did not include the $170 million he had received through the sale of my grandfather's empire. The amounts of money the article mentioned were mind-boggling, and the four siblings had benefited for decades. Dad had clearly shared in the wealth early in his life, but he had had nothing left to show for it by the time he was thirty. I have no idea what happened to his money.

In 1992, only two years after Donald's attempt to attach the codicil to my grandfather's will, effectively cutting his siblings out, the four of them suddenly needed one another: after a lifetime of their father's playing them off against one another, they finally had a common purpose—to protect their inheritance from the government. Fred had refused to heed his lawyers' advice to cede control of his empire to his children before his death in order to minimize estate taxes. That meant that Maryanne, Elizabeth, Donald, and Robert would be responsible for potentially hundreds of millions of dollars of estate taxes. In addition to dozens of buildings, my grandfather had amassed extraordinary sums of cash. His properties carried no debt and brought in millions of dollars every year. The siblings' solution was to establish All County Building Supply & Maintenance. At that point, my grandfather was effectively sidelined by his increasing dementia—not that he would have objected to their scheme. And since my father was long gone, Maryanne, Donald, and Robert could do whatever they wanted; they were our trustees, but there was no one to force them to fulfill their obligations to Fritz and me, and they could easily keep us out of the loop.

My aunts and uncles detested paying taxes almost as much as their father did, and it seemed the main purpose of All County was to siphon money from Trump Management through large gifts disguised as "legitimate business transactions," according to the article. The ruse was so effective that, when Fred died in 1999, he had only $1.9 million in cash and no assets larger than a $10.3 million IOU from Donald. After Gam's death the following year, the combined value of my grandparents' estate was said to be just $51.8 million, a laughable assertion, especially since the siblings sold the empire for more than $700 million four years later.

My grandfather's investment in Donald had been extremely successful in the short term. He had strategically deployed millions of dollars, and often tens of millions of dollars, at key moments in Donald's "career." Sometimes the funds had supported the image and the lifestyle that came with it; sometimes they had bought Donald access and favors. With increasing frequency, they had bailed him out. In that way, Fred purchased the ability to bask in Donald's reflected glory, satisfied with the knowledge that none of it would have been possible without his expertise and largesse. In the long run, however, my grandfather, who had one wish—that his empire survive in perpetuity—lost everything.

Whenever my brother and I met with Robert to discuss my grandfather's estate, he was emphatic about honoring my grandfather's wish that we get nothing. When it came to their own benefit, however, the four surviving Trump siblings had no compunction about doing the one thing my grandfather least would have wanted: when Donald announced his desire to sell, nobody put up a fight.

In 2004, the vast majority of the empire my grandfather had spent more than seven decades building was sold to a single buyer, Ruby Schron, for $705.6 million. The banks financing the sale for Schron had assigned a value of almost $1 billion to the properties, so in one fell swoop my uncle Donald, the master dealmaker, left almost $300 million on the table.

Selling the estate in bulk was a strategic disaster. The smartest thing would have been to keep Trump Management intact. With practically no effort on their part, the four siblings could have earned $5 million to $10 million a year *each*. But Donald needed a much bigger infusion of cash. Such a paltry sum—even if it came to him annually—wasn't going to cut it.

They could also have sold the buildings and complexes individually. That would have added substantially to the selling price. That process, though, would have been a lengthy one. Donald, whose Atlantic City creditors were nipping at his heels, didn't want to wait. Besides, it would have been almost impossible to keep the news of dozens of sales a secret. They needed to complete the sale in one transaction, as quickly and as quietly as possible.

They succeeded on that score. It may be the only one of Donald's real estate deals that received no press attention. Whatever objections Maryanne, Elizabeth, and Robert might have had, they kept to themselves. Even now Maryanne, almost ten years older, smarter, and more accomplished than the second youngest Trump child, deferred to him. "Donald always got his way," she said. Besides, none of them could risk waiting; they all knew where the bodies were buried because they had buried them together in All County.

Split four ways, they each got approximately $170 million. For

Donald, it still wasn't enough. Maybe it wasn't for any of them. Nothing ever was.

When I visited Maryanne in September 2018, less than a month before the article was published, she mentioned that she had been contacted by David Barstow. My cousin David, who had tracked my grandfather's old accountant Jack Mitnick, now ninety-one, to a nursing home somewhere in Florida, believed he must have been the source of the exposé. Maryanne brushed the whole thing off and suggested that the article was merely about the 1990 codicil controversy. If she did speak to Barstow, though, she must have known the extent of what they were looking into—All County, the potential tax fraud—but she seemed unfazed by it. I wondered, now for completely different reasons, why she and Robert hadn't tried everything in their power to dissuade Donald from running for president. They couldn't possibly have thought that he (and by extension they) would continue to escape scrutiny.

I met with Maryanne again shortly after the article ran. She denied all of it. She was just a "girl," after all. When a piece of paper requiring her signature had been put in front of her, she'd signed it, no questions asked. "This article goes back sixty years. You know that's before I was a judge," she said, as if the investigation had also *ended* sixty years before. She seemed unconcerned that there would be any repercussions. Although a court inquiry had been opened into her alleged conduct, all she had had to do to put an end to it was retire, which she did, thereby retaining her $200,000-a-year pension.

In the interim, she had transferred her suspicion from the geriatric Jack Mitnick to her first cousin John Walter, my grandfather's sister Elizabeth's son, who had died that January. I marveled at the ease with which Maryanne jumped to that conclusion. John had worked for and with my grandfather for decades, had benefited enormously from his uncle's wealth, had been heavily involved in All County, and, as far as I knew, had always been very loyal. I thought it strange she would implicate him—although her suspicions of him worked in my favor. What I didn't know at the time was that John's obituary had neglected to mention Donald. John had always been interested in Trump family history and boastful of his connection with Trump Management, so that was a remarkable omission.

More surprising, though, was the fact that Maryanne didn't seem to think that I would find anything in the article disturbing—as if she, too, had come to believe a version of events that obliterated the truth and rewrote history. It didn't occur to her that the revelations would affect me in any way.

In fact, the vast amounts of money the siblings had possibly stolen made their fight with us over my grandfather's will and their drastic devaluation of our partnership share (which I now understood for the first time) seem pathologically petty and their treatment of my nephew vis-à-vis our medical insurance even more cruel.

CHAPTER FOURTEEN

A Civil Servant in Public Housing

There is a through line from the House to the Trump Tower triplex to the West Wing, just as there is from Trump Management to the Trump Organization to the Oval Office. The first are essentially controlled environments in which Donald's material needs have always been taken care of; the second, a series of sinecures in which the work was done by others and Donald never needed to acquire expertise in order to attain or retain power (which partly explains his disdain for the expertise of others). All of this has protected Donald from his own failures while allowing him to believe himself a success.

Donald was to my grandfather what the border wall has been for Donald: a vanity project funded at the expense of more worthy pursuits. Fred didn't groom Donald to succeed him; when he was in his right mind, he wouldn't trust Trump Management to anybody. Instead, he used Donald, despite his failures and poor judgment, as the public face of his own thwarted ambition. Fred kept propping up Donald's false sense of accomplishment until the only asset Donald had was the ease with which he could be duped by more powerful men.

There was a long line of people willing to take advantage of him. In the 1980s, New York journalists and gossip columnists discovered that Donald couldn't distinguish between mockery and flattery and used his shamelessness to sell papers. That image, and the weakness of the man it represented, were precisely what appealed to Mark Burnett. By 2004, when *The Apprentice* first aired, Donald's finances were a mess (even with his $170 million cut of my grandfather's estate when he and his siblings sold the properties), and his own "empire" consisted of increasingly desperate branding opportunities such as Trump Steaks, Trump Vodka, and Trump University. That made him an easy target for Burnett. Both Donald and the viewers were the butt of the joke that was *The Apprentice*, which, despite all evidence to the contrary, presented him as a legitimately successful tycoon.

For the first forty years of his real estate career, my grandfather never acquired debt. In the 1970s and '80s, however, all of that changed as Donald's ambitions grew larger and his missteps became more frequent. Far from expanding his father's empire, everything Donald did after Trump Tower (which, along with his first project, the Grand Hyatt, could never have been accomplished without Fred's money and influence) chipped away at the empire's value. By the late 1980s, the Trump Organization seemed to be in the business of losing money, as Donald siphoned untold millions away from Trump Management in order to support the growing myth of himself as a real estate phenom and master dealmaker.

Ironically, as Donald's failures in real estate grew, so did my grandfather's need for him to appear successful. Fred surrounded Donald with people who knew what they were doing while giving him the credit; who propped him up and lied for him; who knew how the family business worked.

The more money my grandfather threw at Donald, the more confidence Donald had, which led him to pursue bigger and riskier projects, which led to greater failures, forcing Fred to step in with more help. By continuing to enable Donald, my grandfather kept making him worse: more needy for media attention and free money, more self-aggrandizing and delusional about his "greatness."

Although bailing out Donald was originally Fred's exclusive domain, it didn't take long for the banks to become partners in the project. At first, taken in by what they believed to be Donald's ruthless efficiency and ability to get a job done, they were operating in good faith. As the bankruptcies piled up and the bills for the reckless purchases came due, the loans continued but now as a means to maintain the illusion of success that had fooled them in the first place. It's understandable that Donald increasingly felt he had the upper hand, even if he didn't. He was completely unaware that other people were using him for their own ends and believed that he was in control. Fred, the banks, and the media gave him more leeway in order to get him to do their bidding.

In the very early stages of his attempts to take over the Commodore Hotel, Donald held a press conference presenting his involvement in the project as a fait accompli. He lied about transactions that hadn't taken place, inserting himself in a way that made it difficult for him to be removed. He and Fred then used this gambit to leverage his newly inflated reputation in the New York press—and many millions of dollars of my grandfather's money—to get enormous tax abatements for his next development, Trump Tower.

In Donald's mind, he has accomplished everything on his own merits, cheating notwithstanding. How many interviews has he given in which he offers the obvious falsehood that his father loaned him a mere million dollars that he had to pay back but he was otherwise solely responsible for his success? It's easy to understand why he would believe this. Nobody has failed upward as consistently and spectacularly as the ostensible leader of the shrinking free world.

Donald today is much as he was at three years old: incapable of growing, learning, or evolving, unable to regulate his emotions, moderate his responses, or take in and synthesize information.

Donald's need for affirmation is so great that he doesn't seem to notice that the largest group of his supporters are people he wouldn't condescend to be seen with outside of a rally. His deep-seated insecurities have created in him a black hole of need that constantly requires the light of compliments that disappears as soon as he's soaked it in.

Nothing is ever enough. This is far beyond garden-variety narcissism; Donald is not simply weak, his ego is a fragile thing that must be bolstered every moment because he knows deep down that he is nothing of what he claims to be. He knows he has never been loved. So he must draw you in if he can by getting you to assent to even the most seemingly insignificant thing: "Isn't this plane great?" "Yes, Donald, this plane is great." It would be rude to begrudge him that small concession. Then he makes his vulnerabilities and insecurities your responsibility: you must assuage them, you must take care of him. Failing to do so leaves a vacuum that is unbearable for him to withstand for long. If you're someone who cares about his approval, you'll say anything to retain it. He has suffered mightily, and if you aren't doing all you can to alleviate that suffering, you should suffer, too.

From his childhood in the House to his early forays into the New York real estate world and high society until today, Donald's aberrant behavior has been consistently normalized by others. When he hit the New York real estate scene, he was touted as a brash, self-made dealmaker. "Brash" was applied to him as a compliment (used to imply self-assertiveness more than rudeness or arrogance), and he was neither self-made nor a good dealmaker. But that was how it started—with his misuse of language and the media's failure to ask pointed questions.

His real skills (self-aggrandizement, lying, and sleight of hand) were interpreted as strengths unique to his brand of success. By perpetuating his version of the story he wanted told about his wealth and his subsequent "successes," our family and then many others started the process of normalizing Donald. His hiring (and treatment) of undocumented workers and his refusal to pay contractors for completed work were assumed to be the cost of doing business. Treating people with disrespect and nickel-and-diming them made him look tough.

Those misrepresentations must have seemed harmless at the time—a way to sell more copies of the *New York Post* or increase the viewership of *Inside Edition*—but each transgression inevitably led to another, more serious one. The idea that his tactics were legitimate calculations instead of unethical cons was yet another aspect of the myth that he and my grandfather had been constructing for decades.

Though Donald's fundamental nature hasn't changed, since his inauguration the amount of stress he's under *has* changed dramatically. It's not the stress of the job, because he isn't doing the job—unless watching TV and tweeting insults count. It's the effort to keep the rest of us distracted from the fact that he knows nothing—about politics, civics, or simple human decency—that requires an enormous amount of work. For decades, he has gotten publicity, good and bad, but he's rarely been subjected to close scrutiny, and he's never had to face significant opposition. His entire sense of himself and the world is being questioned.

Donald's problems are accumulating because the maneuvering required to solve them, or to pretend they don't exist, has become more complicated, requiring many more people to execute the cover-ups. Donald is completely unprepared to solve his own problems or adequately cover his tracks. After all, the systems were set up in the first place to protect him from his own weaknesses, not help him negotiate the wider world.

The walls of his very expensive and well-guarded padded cell are starting to disintegrate. The people with access to him are weaker than Donald is, more craven, but just as desperate. Their futures are directly dependent on his success and favor. They either fail to see or refuse to believe that their fate will be the same as that of anyone who pledged loyalty to him in the past. There seems to be an endless number of people willing to join the claque that protects Donald from his own inadequacies while perpetuating his unfounded belief in himself. Although more powerful people put Donald into the institutions that have shielded him since the very beginning, it's people weaker than he is who are keeping him there.

When Donald became a serious contender for the Republican Party nomination and then the nominee, the national media treated his pathologies (his mendacity, his delusional grandiosity), as well as his racism and misogyny, as if they were entertaining idiosyncrasies beneath which lurked maturity and seriousness of purpose. Over time, the vast bulk of the Republican Party—from the extreme Right to the so-called moderates—either embraced him or, in order to use his weakness and malleability to their own advantage, looked the other way.

After the election, Vladimir Putin, Kim Jong-un, and Mitch Mc-Connell, all of whom bear more than a passing psychological resemblance to Fred, recognized in a way others should have but did not that Donald's checkered personal history and his unique personality flaws make him extremely vulnerable to manipulation by smarter, more powerful men. His pathologies have rendered him so simple-minded that it takes nothing more than repeating to him the things he says to and about himself dozens of times a day—he's the smartest, the greatest, the best—to get him to do whatever they want, whether it's imprisoning children in concentration camps, betraying allies, implementing economy-crushing tax cuts, or degrading every institution that's contributed to the United States' rise and the flourishing of liberal democracy.

In an article for *The Atlantic*, Adam Serwer wrote that, for Donald, the cruelty is the point. For Fred, that was entirely true. One of the few pleasures my grandfather had, aside from making money, was humiliating others. Convinced of his rightness in all situations, buoyed by his stunning success and a belief in his superiority, he had to punish any challenge to his authority swiftly and decisively and put the challenger in his place. That was effectively what happened when Fred promoted Donald over Freddy to be president of Trump Management.

Unlike my grandfather, Donald has always struggled for legitimacy—

as an adequate replacement for Freddy, as a Manhattan real estate developer or casino tycoon, and now as the occupant of the Oval Office who can never escape the taint of being utterly without qualification or the sense that his "win" was illegitimate. Over Donald's lifetime, as his failures mounted despite my grandfather's repeated—and extravagant—interventions, his struggle for legitimacy, which could never be won, turned into a scheme to make sure nobody found out that he's never been legitimate at all. This has never been more true than it is now, and it is exactly the conundrum our country finds itself in: the government as it is currently constituted, including the executive branch, half of Congress, and the majority of the Supreme Court, is entirely in the service of protecting Donald's ego; that has become almost its entire purpose.

His cruelty serves, in part, as a means to distract both us and himself from the true extent of his failures. The more egregious his failures become, the more egregious his cruelty becomes. Who can pay attention to the children he's kidnapped and put into concentration camps on the Mexican border when he's threatening to out whistleblowers, coercing senators to acquit him in the face of overwhelming evidence of guilt, and pardoning Navy SEAL Eddie Gallagher, who'd been accused of war crimes and convicted of posing for a picture with a corpse, all within the same month? If he can keep forty-seven thousand spinning plates in the air, nobody can focus on any one of them. So there's that: it's just a distraction.

His cruelty is also an exercise of his power, such as it is. He has always wielded it against people who are weaker than he is or who are constrained by their duty or dependence from fighting back. Employees and political appointees can't fight back when he attacks them in his Twitter feed because to do so would risk their jobs or their reputations. Freddy couldn't retaliate when his little brother mocked his passion for flying because of his filial responsibility and his decency, just as governors in blue states, desperate to get adequate help for their citizens during the COVID-19 crisis, are constrained from calling out

Donald's incompetence for fear he would withhold ventilators and other supplies needed in order to save lives. Donald learned a long time ago how to pick his targets.

Donald continues to exist in the dark space between the fear of indifference and the fear of failure that led to his brother's destruction. It took forty-two years for the destruction to be completed, but the foundations were laid early and played out before Donald's eyes as he was experiencing his own trauma. The combination of those two things—what he witnessed and what he experienced—both isolated him and terrified him. The role that fear played in his childhood and the role it plays now can't be overstated. And the fact that fear continues to be an overriding emotion for him speaks to the hell that must have existed inside the House six decades ago.

Every time you hear Donald talking about how something is the greatest, the best, the biggest, the most tremendous (the implication being that he made them so), you have to remember that the man speaking is still, in essential ways, the same little boy who is desperately worried that he, like his older brother, is inadequate and that he, too, will be destroyed for his inadequacy. At a very deep level, his bragging and false bravado are not directed at the audience in front of him but at his audience of one: his long-dead father.

Donald has always been able to get away with making blanket statements ("I know more about [fill in the blank] than anybody, believe me" or the other iteration, "Nobody knows more about [fill in the blank] than me"); he's been allowed to riff about nuclear weapons, trade with China, and other things about which he knows nothing; he's gone essentially unchallenged when touting the efficacy of drugs for the treatment of COVID-19 that have not been tested or engaging in an absurd, revisionist history in which he's never made a mistake and nothing is his fault.

It's easy to sound coherent and somewhat knowledgeable when

you control the narrative and are never pressed to elaborate on your premise or demonstrate that you actually understand the underlying facts. It is an indictment (among many) of the media that none of that changed during the campaign, when exposing Donald's lies and outrageous claims might actually have saved us from his presidency. On the few occasions he was asked about his positions and policies (which for all intents and purposes don't really exist), he still wasn't expected or required to make sense or demonstrate any depth of understanding. Since the election, he's figured out how to avoid such questions completely; White House press briefings and formal news conferences have been replaced with "chopper talk" during which he can pretend he can't hear any unwelcome questions over the noise of the helicopter blades. In 2020, his pandemic "press briefings" quickly devolved into mini–campaign rallies filled with self-congratulation, demagoguery, and ring kissing. In them he has denied the unconscionable failures that have already killed thousands, lied about the progress that's being made, and scapegoated the very people who are risking their lives to save us despite being denied adequate protection and equipment by his administration. Even as hundreds of thousands of Americans are sick and dying, he spins it as a victory, as proof of his stunning leadership. And in the event that anybody thinks he's capable of being serious or somber, he'll throw in a joke about bedding models or lie about the size of his Facebook following for good measure. Still the news networks refuse to pull away. The few journalists who do challenge him, and even those who simply ask Donald for words of comfort for a terrified nation, are derided and dismissed as "nasty." The through line from Donald's early, destructive behavior that Fred actively encouraged to the media's unwillingness to challenge him and the Republican Party's willingness to turn a blind eye to the daily corruption he has committed since January 20, 2017, have led to the impending collapse of this once great nation's economy, democracy, and health.

We must dispense with the idea of Donald's "strategic brilliance" in understanding the intersection of media and politics. He doesn't have a strategy; he never has. Despite the fluke that was his electoral advantage and a "victory" that was at best suspect and at worst illegitimate, he never had his finger on the pulse of the zeitgeist; his bluster and shamelessness just happened to resonate with certain segments of the population. If what he was doing during the 2016 campaign *hadn't* worked, he would have kept doing it anyway, because lying, playing to the lowest common denominator, cheating, and sowing division are all he knows. He is as incapable of adjusting to changing circumstances as he is of becoming "presidential." He did tap into a certain bigotry and inchoate rage, which he's always been good at doing. The full-page screed he paid to publish in the *New York Times* in 1989 calling for the Central Park Five to be put to death wasn't about his deep concern for the rule of law; it was an easy opportunity for him to take on a deeply serious topic that was very important to the city while sounding like an authority in the influential and prestigious pages of the Gray Lady. It was unvarnished racism meant to stir up racial animosity in a city already seething with it. All five boys, Kevin Richardson, Antron McCray, Raymond Santana, Korey Wise, and Yusef Salaam, were subsequently cleared, proven innocent via incontrovertible DNA evidence. To this day, however, Donald insists that they were guilty—yet another example of his inability to drop a preferred narrative even when it's contradicted by established fact.

Donald takes any rebuke as a challenge and doubles down on the behavior that drew fire in the first place, as if the criticism is permission to do worse. Fred came to appreciate Donald's obstinacy because it signaled the kind of toughness he sought in his sons. Fifty years later, people are literally dying because of his catastrophic decisions and disastrous inaction. With millions of lives at stake, he takes accusations about the federal government's failure to provide ventilators personally, threatening to withhold funding and lifesaving equipment from states whose governors don't pay sufficient homage to him. That doesn't surprise me. The deafening silence in response to such a blatant display of sociopathic disregard for human life or the consequences for one's actions, on the other hand, fills me with despair and reminds me that Donald isn't really the problem after all.

This is the end result of Donald's having continually been given a pass and rewarded not just for his failures but for his transgressions—against tradition, against decency, against the law, and against fellow human beings. His acquittal in the sham Senate impeachment trial was another such reward for bad behavior.

The lies may become true in his mind as soon as he utters them, but they're still lies. It's just another way for him to see what he can get away with. And so far, he's gotten away with everything.

The Tenth Circle

On November 9, 2016, my despair was triggered in part by the certainty that Donald's cruelty and incompetence would get people killed. My best guess at the time was that that would occur through a disaster of his own making, such as an avoidable war he either provoked or stumbled into. I couldn't have anticipated how many people would willingly enable his worst instincts, which have resulted in government-sanctioned kidnapping of children, detaining of refugees at the border, and betrayal of our allies, among other atrocities. And I couldn't have foreseen that a global pandemic would present itself, allowing him to display his grotesque indifference to the lives of other people.

Donald's initial response to COVID-19 underscores his need to minimize negativity at all costs. Fear—the equivalent of weakness in our family—is as unacceptable to him now as it was when he was three years old. When Donald is in the most trouble, superlatives are no longer enough: both the situation and his reactions to it must be unique, even if absurd or nonsensical. On his watch, no hurricane has ever been as wet as Hurricane Maria. "Nobody could have predicted" a pandemic that his own Department of Health and Human Services was running simulations for just a few months before COVID-19 struck in Washington state. Why does he do this? Fear.

Donald didn't drag his feet in December 2019, in January, in February, in March because of his narcissism; he did it because of his fear of appearing weak or failing to project the message that everything was "great," "beautiful," and "perfect." The irony is that his failure to face the truth has inevitably led to massive failure anyway. In this case, the lives of potentially hundreds of thousands of people will be lost and the economy of the richest country in history may well be destroyed. Donald will acknowledge none of this, moving the goalposts to hide the evidence and convincing himself in the process that he's done a better job than anybody else could have if only a few hundred thousand die instead of 2 million.

"Get even with people who have screwed you," Donald has said, but often the person he's getting revenge on is somebody he screwed over first—such as the contractors he's refused to pay or the niece and nephew he refused to protect. Even when he manages to hit his target, his aim is so bad that he causes collateral damage. Andrew Cuomo, the governor of New York and currently the de facto leader of the country's COVID-19 response, has committed not only the sin of insufficiently kissing Donald's ass but the *ultimate* sin of showing Donald up by being better and more competent, a real leader who is respected and effective and admired. Donald can't fight back by shutting Cuomo up or reversing his decisions; having abdicated his authority to lead a nationwide response, he no longer has the ability to counter decisions made at the state level. Donald can insult Cuomo and complain about him, but every day the governor's real leadership further reveals Donald as a petty, pathetic little man—ignorant, incapable, out of his depth, and lost in his own delusional spin. What Donald *can* do in order to offset the powerlessness and rage he feels is punish the rest of us. He'll withhold ventilators or steal supplies from states that have not groveled sufficiently. If New York continues not to have enough equipment, Cuomo will look bad, the rest of us be damned. Thankfully, Donald doesn't have many supporters in New York City, but even some of those will die because of his craven need for "revenge." What Donald thinks is justified retaliation is, in this context, mass murder.

It would have been easy for Donald to be a hero. People who have hated and criticized him would have forgiven or overlooked his endless stream of appalling actions if he'd simply had somebody take the pandemic preparedness manual down from the shelf where it was put after the Obama administration gave it to him. If he'd alerted the appropriate agencies and state governments at the first evidence the virus was highly contagious, had extremely high mortality rates, and was not being contained. If he'd invoked the Defense Production Act of 1950 to begin production of PPE, ventilators, and other necessary equipment to prepare the country to deal with the worst-case scenario. If he'd allowed medical and scientific experts to give daily press conferences during which facts were presented clearly and honestly. If he'd ensured that there was a systematic, top-down approach and coordination among all of the necessary agencies. Most of those tasks would have required almost no effort on his part. All he would have had to do was make a couple of phone calls, give a speech or two, then delegate everything else. He might have been accused of being too cautious, but most of us would have been safe and many more of us would have survived. Instead, states are forced to buy vital supplies from private contractors; the federal government commandeers those supplies, and then FEMA distributes them back to private contractors, who then resell them.

While thousands of Americans die alone, Donald touts stock market gains. As my father lay dying alone, Donald went to the movies. If he can in any way profit from your death, he'll facilitate it, and then he'll ignore the fact that you died.

Why did it take so long for Donald to act? Why didn't he take the novel coronavirus seriously? In part because, like my grandfather, he has no imagination. The pandemic didn't immediately have to do with him, and managing the crisis in every moment doesn't help him promote his preferred narrative that no one has ever done a better job than he has.

As the pandemic moved into its third, then fourth month, and the death toll continued its rise into the tens of thousands, the press started to comment on Donald's lack of empathy for those who have died and the families they leave behind. The simple fact is that Donald is fundamentally incapable of acknowledging the suffering of others. Telling the stories of those we've lost would *bore* him. Acknowledging the victims of COVID-19 would be to associate himself with their weakness, a trait his father taught him to despise. Donald can no more advocate for the sick and dying than he could put himself between his father and Freddy. Perhaps most crucially, for Donald there is no value in empathy, no tangible upside to caring for other people. David Corn wrote, "Everything is transactional for this poor broken human being. Everything." It is an epic tragedy of parental failure that my uncle does not understand that he or anybody else has intrinsic worth.

In Donald's mind, even acknowledging an inevitable threat would indicate weakness. Taking responsibility would open him up to blame. Being a hero—being good—is impossible for him.

The same could be said of his handling of the worst civil unrest since the assassination of Martin Luther King, Jr. This is another crisis in which it would have been so easy for Donald to triumph, but his ignorance overwhelms his ability to turn to his advantage the third national catastrophe to occur on his watch. An effective response would have entailed a call for unity, but Donald requires division. It is the only way he knows how to survive—my grandfather ensured that decades ago when he turned his children against each other.

I can only imagine the envy with which Donald watched Derek Chauvin's casual cruelty and monstrous indifference as he murdered George Floyd; hands in his pockets, his insouciant gaze aimed at the camera. I can only imagine that Donald wishes it had been his knee on Floyd's neck.

Instead, Donald withdraws to his comfort zones—Twitter, Fox News—casting blame from afar, protected by a figurative or literal bunker. He rants about the weakness of others even as he demonstrates his own. But he can never escape the fact that he is and always will be a terrified little boy.

Donald's monstrosity is the manifestation of the very weakness within him that he's been running from his entire life. For him, there has never been any option but to be positive, to project strength, no matter how illusory, because doing anything else carries a death sentence; my father's short life is evidence of that. The country is now suffering from the same toxic positivity that my grandfather deployed specifically to drown out his ailing wife, torment his dying son, and damage past healing the psyche of his favorite child, Donald J. Trump.

"Everything's great. Right, Toots?"

Acknowledgments

At Simon & Schuster, thanks to Jon Karp, Eamon Dolan, Jessica Chin, Paul Dippolito, Lynn Anderson, and Jackie Seow.

At WME thanks to Jay Mandel and Sian-Ashleigh Edwards.

Thank you also to Carolyn Levin for your thoughtful vetting; David Corn at *Mother Jones* for your kindness; Darren Ankrom, fact-checker extraordinaire; Stuart Oltchick for telling me about better days; Captain Jerry Lawler for all of the wonderful TWA history; and Maryanne Trump Barry for all of the enlightening information.

My appreciation to Denise Kemp for the solidarity with me; to my mother, Linda Trump, for all of the great stories; Laura Schweers; Debbie R; Stefanie B; and Jennifer T for your friendship and trust when I most needed them. Jill and Mark Nass for helping us keep the tradition alive (JCE!).

To our beloved Trumpy, whom I miss every day.

I am deeply grateful to Ted Boutrous, for that first meeting and for believing in the cause; Annie Champion for your generosity and friendship; Pat Roth for your thoughtful feedback and for being in my life; Annamaria Forcier for being such a good friend to my dad, I am so glad I found you; Susanne Craig and Russ Buettner for their extraordinary journalism and integrity, thank you for bringing me along for the ride. Sue, none of this would have been possible without your persistence, courage, and encouragement; Liz Stein for being on the journey with me and making this a better book—and this a much more fun, less lonely experience than it might have been (and, of course, for Baby Yoda); Eric Adler for being there for me throughout, for your tireless feedback, and for having my back at the local pawnbroker; and Alice Frankston for being involved from the very beginning of this project, believing in it even when I didn't, and reading every word more times than I can count. I can't wait for what comes next.

And finally, to my daughter, Avary, for being more patient and understanding than any kid should have to be. I love you.

Index

About the Author

Mary L. Trump holds a PhD from the Derner Institute of Advanced Psychological Studies and taught graduate courses in trauma, psychopathology, and developmental psychology. She lives with her daughter in New York.